PSYCHOLOGY

Why We Smile, Strive, and Sing

Julie K. Rubini

Illustrated by Tom Casteel

Nomad Press

A division of Nomad Communications

10 9 8 7 6 5 4 3 2 1

This book was manufactured by Versa Press, Inc., East Peoria, Illinois
June 2020, Job #J20-01721
ISBN Softcover: 978-1-61930-911-1
ISBN Hardcover: 978-1-61930-908-1

Educational Consultant, Marla Conn

Questions regarding the ordering of this book should be addressed to
Nomad Press
2456 Christian St., White River Junction, VT 05001
www.nomadpress.net

Printed in the United States.

Titles in the Inquire & Investigate
Human Beings set

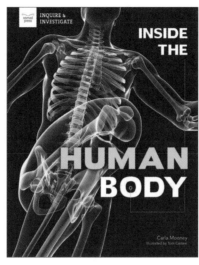

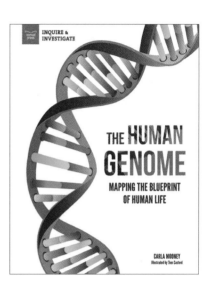

Check out more titles at www.nomadpress.net

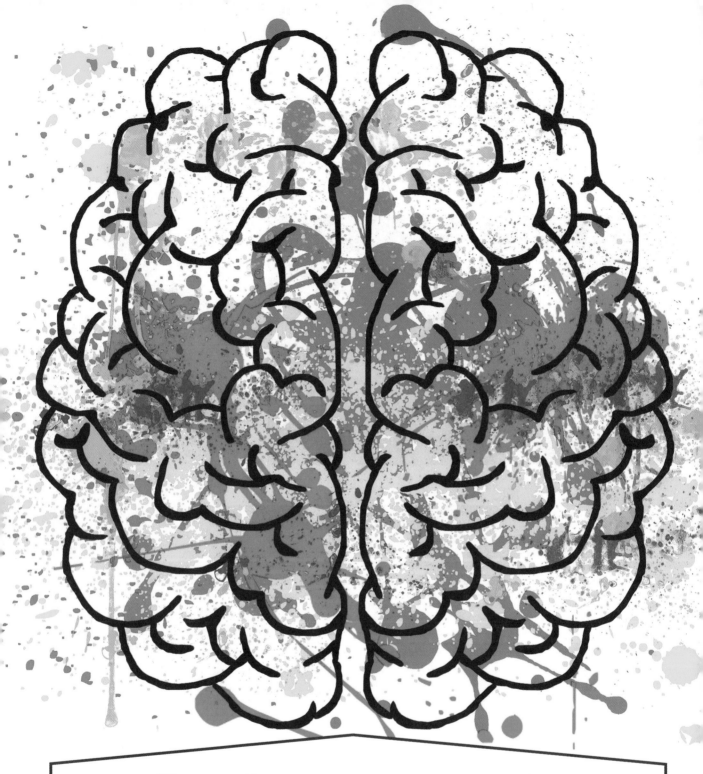

Interested in primary sources?

Look for this icon.

You can use a smartphone or tablet app to scan the QR codes and explore more! Cover up neighboring QR codes to make sure you're scanning the right one. You can find a list of URLs on the Resources page.

If the QR code doesn't work, try searching the internet with the Keyword Prompts to find other helpful sources.

🔎 human behavior

Contents

TIMELINE

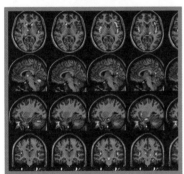

Fourth century BCE: Often regarded as the father of psychology, Aristotle writes his book, *De Anima* (*On the Soul*), the first book of psychology.

1600s: René Descartes formulates the connection between the mind and the body.

1859: Charles Darwin proposes in his book, *On the Origin of the Species,* that all of our traits are inherited.

1872: Charles Darwin publishes *The Expression of the Emotions in Men and Animals*, suggesting that behaviors are adapted through evolution.

1879: Dr. Wilhelm Wundt establishes the first laboratory of experimental psychology in Germany.

1905: Mary Whiton Calkins becomes the first female president of both the American Psychological Association and the American Philosophical Association.

1920: Dr. John B. Watson conducts his infamous "Little Albert" experiments.

1920: Dr. Francis Cecil Sumner becomes the first African American to receive a Ph.D. in psychology.

1923: Melanie Klein, considered one of the founding figures in psychoanalysis, analyzes her first child patient.

1939: Mamie Katherine Phipps Clark uses black and white dolls to study racial awareness in African American preschool children and finds they tend to select the white dolls.

1948: Dr. Burrhus Frederic (B.F.) Skinner creates the Skinner Box and experiments with rats to support his theories on the impact of the environment on behavior.

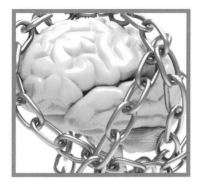

1960: Dr. Walter Mischel at Stanford University conducts the "Marshmallow Effect" experiments on delayed gratification.

1961: Dr. Albert Bandura conducts the Bobo doll experiments to support his hypothesis that childhood aggression is a learned behavior.

1967: Dr. Diana Blumberg Baumrind publishes a paper on the research she conducted, describing three different parenting styles.

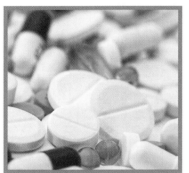

1977: Dr. Gordon G. Gallup presents his research on the freeze response in "fight, flight, or freeze" in an article published in *The Psychological Record*.

1991: Functional magnetic resonance imaging (fMRI) begins to be used on humans.

2013: The term "fear of missing out," or FOMO, is added to the *Oxford English Dictionary*.

2013: The Pew Research Center releases a study on impacts of internet use and social media on stress levels.

2015: Two studies of adults 65 years and older report a link between loneliness and mental and physical debilitation.

2016: More than 190 researchers around the world analyze data on 300,000 people and determine there are genetic links to happiness and depression.

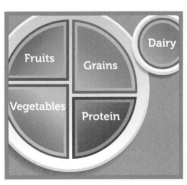

2019: Researchers at the University of Illinois at Chicago identify brain circuitry differences that might be associated with suicidal behavior with individuals with mood disorders.

Introduction ▶

What Is Human Psychology?

What are some things that influence human behavior?

Human behavior is incredibly complex and many different factors contribute to it, including the brain, genetics, hormones, environment, and more!

When you feel anxious about a test, do you stay up late studying or do you stay up late playing video games, figuring you're going to fail anyway? If you witness a group of friends bullying a new kid at school, do you join in or step up? Do you prefer to spend a lot of time on your own or do you like to be constantly surrounded by other people?

All of your decisions, actions, and reactions are part of what we study when we learn about psychology. Human behavior is a fascinating subject—it's all about you and how you fit into the world.

Psychology also studies what people do in response to certain stimuli.

Why does one person react to test anxiety by studying harder while another person assumes they'll do badly and gives up? What makes one person join a group doing the wrong thing as another person steps in to do what is right?

Test anxiety!

Behavior depends on many things—childhood experiences and upbringing, genetics, hormones, the actions of your peers, and your own special blend of attitudes and values. But it all starts with your brain!

WHERE IT ALL BEGINS

The brain is at the center of your thoughts, actions, and responses to situations. The brain is where you process the consequences of your behavior. Are you feeling nervous, excited, sad, or satisfied? You can thank your brain.

Scientists did not always realize that the brain was critical to the study of human behavior. Many early cultures believed that thoughts and feelings originated in other organs, such as the heart, stomach, or lungs.

The Project for Babies is a series of five educational videos about brain development. Check it out! What repercussions does an individual's brain development have on the larger society?

 CEED project babies

In ancient Egypt, embalmers tossed out the brains of dead people as they prepared bodies for burial, but carefully preserved the heart, which they believed was the source of a person's good or evil temperament. The famous ancient Greek philosopher Aristotle (384–322 BCE) thought the brain served only as a kind of temperature control device to keep the body's heat regulated—but it does much more!

It wasn't until 1649 that a French philosopher named René Descartes (1596–1650) announced that the brain had some control over behavior. However, he believed animal spirits in the brain were responsible for most higher mental processes.

> Eventually, people began to notice that behavior and personality sometimes changed after a head injury. Perhaps there was a link between the brain and a person's thoughts, feelings, and reactions!

It was difficult to study the brains of living people before the invention of today's technology. German physician Franz Joseph Gall (1758–1828) leaped over this hurdle in 1796 by concluding that a person's skull was reflective of their character. Phrenology links certain personality traits with specific areas of a person's head. All one had to do to know a person's behavior was to feel the lumps and bumps under their hair.

After gaining popularity for a time in the 1800s, the practice of phrenology was debunked. It was an important step in the development of modern neuroscience and psychology, however. People were beginning to think more critically about the links between behavior and the brain.

PRIMARY SOURCES

(PS)

Primary sources come from people who were eyewitnesses to events. They might write about the event, take pictures, post short messages to social media or blogs, or record the event for radio or video. The photographs in this book are primary sources, taken at the time of the event. Paintings of events are usually not primary sources, since they were often painted long after the event took place.

What other primary sources can you find? Why are primary sources important? Do you learn differently from primary sources than from secondary sources, which come from people who did not directly experience the event?

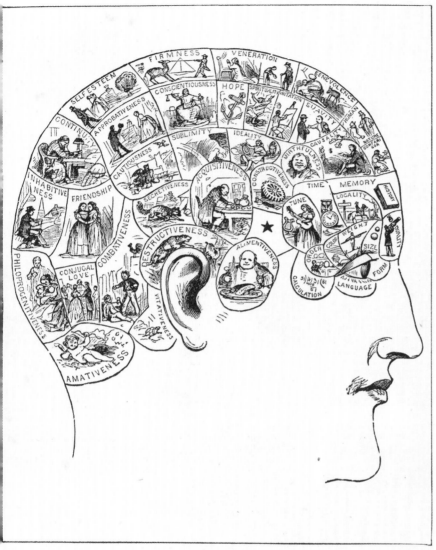

Phrenological Chart of the Faculties.

From *People's Cyclopedia of Universal Knowledge*, 1883

THE FATHER OF MODERN PSYCHOLOGY

Wilhelm Wundt (1832–1920) is thought of as the father of modern psychology. He established the world's first experimental psychology lab in Germany in 1879. Before this, psychology was considered to be part of the study of philosophy, which meant people didn't perform scientific experiments to study behavior. Instead, they used rational analysis, a form of thinking and discussing subjects that doesn't include applying rigorous scientific testing. This changed as psychology began to be considered an actual science that required experimentation, observation, reproduction of results, and collaboration.

Head injuries still provided the most information for scientists through the nineteenth century. After the person died, their brain could be removed and studied for clues as to how the injury had changed the person's behavior.

PHINEAS GAGE

In 1848, an American railroad worker named Phineas Gage (1823–1860) was injured when an explosion sent a large iron rod through his head. Much of his brain's left frontal lobe was damaged in the accident. Although Gage survived, his behavior changed dramatically. Before the accident, Gage was polite and thoughtful. After the accident, he was rude and reckless. Friends of Gage said that he was no longer the same person. Doctors believe that the changes in Gage's personality were a result of brain damage. His case was one of the first to demonstrate that brain damage to the frontal lobes can affect social and moral judgment. Decades later, a reconstruction of Gage's injuries showed that the areas of his brain linked to moral sensitivity were damaged in his accident.

Today, powerful tools help scientists view the brain's detailed anatomy, even in living humans. We are able to create maps of the brain and pinpoint which areas contribute to certain types of behaviors.

The more we know about the brain, the more we know about developing healthy habits, taking care of our psychological health, and treating mental illness.

Phineas Gage, holding the iron rod that hurt him

One interesting thing about your brain is that it changes as you grow and develop, just like the rest of your body. That means the way you think and behave changes, too. The thoughts and reactions you have as a 12-year-old are not going to be the same when you're 16, 25, or 40 years old.

In fact, your prefrontal cortex, one of the areas of your brain that is directly connected with your ability to make judgments, isn't fully developed until you are in your mid-20s. So, if someone asks you, "What were you thinking?" the answer is, quite simply, you weren't! Your brain isn't fully grown yet and can't do some kinds of thinking.

Of course, people younger than 25 are still expected to make good choices.

BEYOND THE BRAIN

External influences are important factors in the development of healthy behavior. Were you exposed to different experiences such as travel and family outings? Did you always have a place to stay at night? Was there always food to eat and people with you to help with homework, fears you might have had, and problems you needed to talk about?

Everyone's early childhood experiences are different. Some young people have caregivers that offer love, trust, and security, while other kids have to seek out people who will fulfill these basic needs. Experiences such as homelessness, hunger, abuse, and grief can all be powerful influences.

SCIENTIFIC METHOD

The scientific method is the process scientists use to ask questions and find answers. Keep a science journal to record your methods and observations during all the activities in this book. You can use a scientific method worksheet to keep your ideas and observations organized.

Question: What are we trying to find out? What problem are we trying to solve?

Research: What is already known about this topic?

Hypothesis: What do we think the answer will be?

Equipment: What supplies are we using?

Method: What procedure are we following?

Results: What happened and why?

PSYCH!

/////////////////////////

Psychology is the science of human behavior. Biology is the science of life. Neurology is the study of the brain. Neuroendocrinology studies the interactions between the nervous system and the endocrine system. All play a role in understanding human behavior.

TEXT TO WORLD

What kinds of behavior do you see from your friends? Does this behavior change in group settings?

Protest gatherings, such as this one in Hong Kong is 2019, offer opportunities to witness human behavior in a group.

Both positive and negative early experiences affect your emotional development. However, the important thing to remember is that people ultimately make choices about behavior, no matter their environment and upbringing.

In addition to brains and environments, there are other influencing factors on behavior.

Has anyone ever blamed your behavior on hormones? Well, they could be right. Everyone is born with hormones, but certain hormones begin to work only when you reach puberty, when your brain experiences them for the first time. Hormones are chemical messengers that travel through your body and have both physical and emotional consequences.

Genetics is another thing that plays a major role in behavior. You are who you are and behave the way you do partly because you were born this way.

Outside the body, whether or not you are surrounded by other people can have an effect on your behavior, too. You might think that how you act when you're alone is how you act all the time. Studies have shown though—and you might have witnessed this yourself at school or other places where there are lots of people—people do have different standards of behavior depending on their surroundings.

In *Psychology*, we'll take a closer look at the brain and how it affects behavior. We'll examine the teenage brain, genes and the environment, behavior in groups, and how we can help ourselves stay emotionally healthy. Psychology is a fascinating science that can teach you a lot about both yourself, your friends, and the world!

VOCAB LAB

There is a lot of new vocabulary in this book. Turn to the glossary in the back when you come to a word you don't understand. Practice your new vocabulary in the VOCAB LAB activities in each chapter.

KEY QUESTIONS

- **What is your own general behavior like, day to day?**
- **What causes a significant reaction in your own behavior? Why?**
- **Why did it take so long for people to make a connection between the brain and behavior?**

HI, I'M . . .

When you meet a new person, what's the first thing you tell them? Usually, it's your name! What might happen if you started with a characteristic instead? Try it and find out! This activity is best at the start of a new school year or in a group where participants don't know each other too well.

- **Everyone walks around the room, introducing themselves to the others.** However, instead of introducing yourselves by name, choose one of these introductions:

  - What you ate for breakfast

  - Your favorite color

  - Your favorite activity

- **For example, someone might say,** "Hi, I'm Instant Breakfast and a banana. Who are you?"

- **Discuss your observations as a group.** What did you notice about people as they introduced themselves this way? What was the most popular choice of introduction? Did the choices seem to fall along gender, age, or other identifying lines? Why might this be so?

> To investigate more, repeat this activity with people who are close and know each other very well. Use different introductions that people might not know about each other. Does anything surprising come up?

VOCAB LAB

Write down what you think each word means. What root words can you find to help you? What does the context of the word tell you?

behavior, **genetics**, **hormones**, **personality**, and **psychology**.

Compare your definitions with those of your friends or classmates. Did you all come up with the same meanings? Turn to the text and glossary if you need help.

Chapter 1 ▶

Behavior and the Brain

How is your brain
connected to
your behavior?

Everything you do starts in the brain! As different nerves relay certain signals to your brain, your behavior changes, whether or not you mean it to change.

Let's say you are walking home from a friend's house. You have your earbuds in and you're listening to music. Across the street, a little kid is riding a bike. You see the boy peddling fast, faster. Then, out of the corner of your eye, you notice he falls. What do you do? Do you instinctively run across the street to see if he's okay? Do you look around to see if his mom is nearby? Or do you wait to see if he gets back on his bike?

Whatever you did, why did you make that choice? As you learned in the Introduction, your behavior stems from a variety of sources. One of the major sources of behavior is your brain. After you noticed the kid on the bike and a second before you chose what to do about it, your brain commanded your muscles to move either toward or away from the situation.

The brain is the glue that holds all the other components of our behavior together. It is where our actions begin.

INSIDE YOUR HEAD

The brain is said to be one of the most complex systems in the universe. Maybe even more complex than the universe itself! The human brain, made up of billions of cells, plays an important role in how you behave and respond to situations.

Your brain is similar to a search engine on your phone or computer. It receives input and processes it. This input is information that you've gathered from the world through your five senses—sight, hearing, touch, taste, and smell. That input travels through your body through bundles of fibers, called nerves. Information travels along your nerves—which are made up of neurons—just as a train travels on a subway line. Subways use electricity to fuel the movement of the train, while neurons are specialized brain cells that move information.

Neurons come in a variety of shapes and sizes, but they all transmit information in the same basic way. They communicate through electrical impulses called action potentials and chemicals called neurotransmitters. The action potential travels through the axon, which is covered in myelin, a substance that helps the information travel more quickly. After traveling along the axon, the action potential ends up at the axon terminal.

Watch this video to see how signals travel through neurons. How many times do you think signals are transmitted through a neuron during the time it took you to watch the clip?

🔍 2-Minute Neuroscience: Neuron

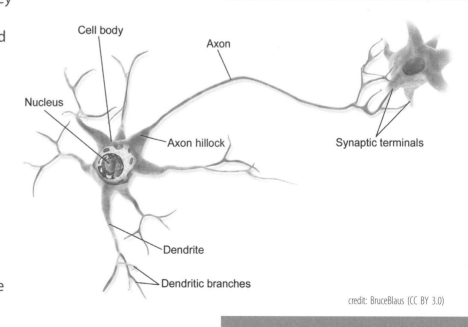

Cell body

Axon

Nucleus

Axon hillock

Synaptic terminals

Dendrite

Dendritic branches

credit: BruceBlaus (CC BY 3.0)

PSYCH!

\\\\\\\\\\\\\\\\\\\\\

Neurons never touch each other. Neurotransmitters relay signals from one neuron to the next through the gap that separates neurons. That gap is a synapse.

I'M SENSING . . .

What area of the brain determines that something tastes salty? Or recognizes that fingers being caught in a door is painful? Or that a room is too hot? It's the parietal lobe that processes sensory information. The parietal lobe regulates the body's five senses—sight, hearing, touch, smell, and taste. This part of the brain is involved in a variety of complex tasks, from recognition and understanding of environmental cues to taking appropriate action. Someone with damage to the parietal lobe might see an object or person, but may not be able to interpret how large the object is or who the person is. They might not move their body to avoid a sharp object or reach out to hug a friend.

Here, the action potential causes the neuron to release the chemical neurotransmitters. These neurotransmitters diffuse across the gaps between neurons called synapses.

Have you ever had to change trains at a train station? An axon terminal is similar to the connecting station. And just as passengers exit out of the train into the station, the information from the axon exits into the axon terminal. Then, a chemical signal causes the information to leave the original neuron and land on the dendrites of the next "listening" neuron. Dendrites, which look like tree branches on the end of the neuron, are receptors that receive signals from other neurons. The process begins again in this neuron.

The incredible neuron messaging system takes place thousands of times during every second of your life.

If the same signals are repeated from neuron to neuron, the synapse connections grow stronger. Think back to traveling on a subway. The first time you are going somewhere, you might get lost and even get off at the wrong station. But the next day, you remember which station you are supposed to get off at. Your memory improves and you learn. The connecting points for the exchange of information, the synapses, have grown stronger.

YOUR BRAIN AND SURVIVAL

At the heart of our behavior is the most elementary behavior of all—survival! We rely on our brain to inform us of the world around us in a way that enables us to stay alive. That might sound dramatic when you think of simply walking through your own town.

But imagine you lived during a time when danger in the form of wild animals lurked everywhere around you. You had to rely on excellent instincts to survive.

Those instincts are formed through your neurons. In ancient times, every time you saw a saber-toothed tiger attack and eat another creature, your neurons applied the concept of danger to that image. That way, you stayed away from the tiger. The same concept of danger might be associated with a certain type of berry that gave you a stomachache when you ate it. Your brain recognizes that certain images mean danger and tells you to avoid them.

Neurons work the same way in today's world. Say you get off a train and someone on the platform starts giving you trouble, taunting you and threatening to take your backpack. Your brain goes through the same process, with those connections between neurons strengthening every time. This is how you learn to avoid dangerous situations. Maybe next time you watch out at that train station for the bully.

Sometimes, your brain learns after the event. Remember when you were little and you accidentally touched a hot stove? The electrical signals from the cells in your fingers traveled to your spinal cord, which reacted by sending its own electrical signal to tell your hand to move away from the heat. It would have taken too long to get instructions from the brain! But your brain's parietal lobe, which processes pain, still learned the lesson—avoid hot stovetops.

We learn from our experiences and through the strengthening of the synaptic connections in our brain. This learning can mean the difference between getting eaten by a predator, taunted by a bully, burning your hand, and more!

The human brain has about 1 quadrillion synapses. That's 1,000,000,000,000,000 synapses! This is equal to about a half-billion synapses per cubic millimeter.

Watch a video about how humans and animals work and remember—and forget—due to activity in the brain. How many neurons are connected in the human brain?

 Thinking Brain mysteries brain

Through experience, the synaptic connections are further developed. Ultimately, we learn to not repeat behavior that might lead to negative consequences.

The brain is like a subway map, with the electrical signals making their way to different stops, or different locations in the brain. To understand better how the circuitry of the brain works, let's explore various areas of the brain and their functions.

THREE SECTIONS OF THE BRAIN

The brain is a complex organ, but at its simplest, it has three sections. These are the cerebrum, the cerebellum, and the brain stem. All perform different functions.

The cerebrum is the most dominant part of the brain. The cerebrum controls your voluntary muscles that do the work you ask them to do. This section of the brain also contains short-term memory. When you are thinking through an algebra problem or figuring out an answer during a biology quiz, your cerebrum is at work for you.

The cerebrum is so big, it is divided into two different sections, or hemispheres, which are separated with a large bundle of nerve fibers called the corpus callosum. Both hemispheres of the brain must work together to help with processing complex information and coordinating physical movement. The corpus callosum serves as a bridge to connect the two brain hemispheres.

The cerebellum is in the back of the brain, below the cerebrum. When riding a bike or zipping along on a skateboard, your cerebellum is in action. It's the section of the brain that is responsible for balance, fine-motor movement such as writing, and coordination.

Cerebral Hemispheres

Right hemisphere   Left hemisphere

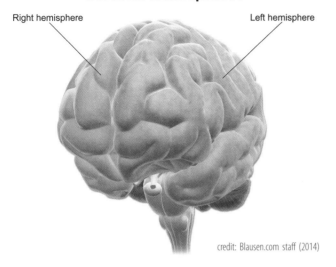

credit: Blausen.com staff (2014)

Whether you are kicking a soccer ball, swinging a tennis racket, or even simply walking across the room, the cerebellum coordinates your muscle activities so these actions can take place smoothly.

The cerebellum is the area of the brain that helps with actions that require practice to improve, such as shooting a basketball through the hoop. This important area of the brain coordinates eye movement.

Breathing is critical to staying alive. This basic function is controlled by the brain stem, the third major section of the brain. The brain stem controls several other basic body functions, including swallowing your food, heart rate, and feeling sleepy or awake.

Within these three major sections of the brain are many smaller areas that control specific things in your body. Let's take a look at some of these, which include four lobes in each hemisphere of the brain.

Take a look at some 3-D views of your brain with the 3D Brain app! Here's an instructional video on how to use the app. With an adult's permission, download the free app to a device.

 YouTube 3D Brain app DNA

Neurobiologists study what is going on in your brain during that split second before you act. Your brain fires up and transmits information to the rest of your body, causing your muscles to move.

HEMISPHERES AND LOBES

Take an apple and cut it in half. Each half represents a hemisphere of the brain. Now, take those apple halves and cut them into quarters. These represent the lobes of the brain. Both hemispheres have four lobes, so separate those apple quarters into two piles to demonstrate the balance of your brain halves.

The four lobes in each hemisphere include the frontal, temporal, parietal, and occipital lobes. Each of the lobes has specific functions, but for our purposes in understanding behavior, the frontal is the most significant. It is the most developed part of the brain, but is also the last part of our brain to fully develop.

Take a look at the main functions of the four different lobes.

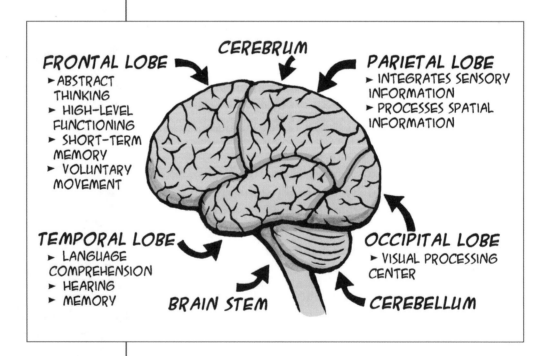

FRONTAL LOBE
- ABSTRACT THINKING
- HIGH-LEVEL FUNCTIONING
- SHORT-TERM MEMORY
- VOLUNTARY MOVEMENT

CEREBRUM

PARIETAL LOBE
- INTEGRATES SENSORY INFORMATION
- PROCESSES SPATIAL INFORMATION

TEMPORAL LOBE
- LANGUAGE COMPREHENSION
- HEARING
- MEMORY

BRAIN STEM

OCCIPITAL LOBE
- VISUAL PROCESSING CENTER

CEREBELLUM

- The frontal lobe controls decision-making, personality, behavior, problem-solving, and the ability to speak.

- The temporal lobe controls language, memory, and the ability to hear.

- The parietal lobe controls your ability to interpret language, sense of touch or pain, and spatial perception.

- The occipital lobe controls how you interpret what you see.

To get a sense of how all the sections of the brain work together, imagine walking by yourself on the way to school. You encounter someone coming in the other direction. How does your brain process this situation?

First, you see the person. Your eyes receive a signal because of the light reflecting off the person walking toward you. Special cells in the back of your eye turn the light into a signal that travels down your optic nerve toward the brain.

> The brain can process an image in under 13 milliseconds!

Once the message that someone is walking toward you registers in your brain, neurons within the occipital lobe begin communicating with each other and reaching out to other areas of the brain to make sense of what you are seeing.

Imagine the person walking toward you calls out as you get closer. When you hear something, the tiny bones in your ear vibrate. This vibration causes an electrical signal to shoot to your brain via the auditory nerve. This nerve carries the signal to the temporal lobe.

The Dana Foundation is committed to advancing brain research and educating the public about the potential of research. Check out these fun brain twisters!

 Dana Found brain tease

PSYCH!
\\\\\\\\\\\\\\\\\\\\\\\\\

The average human brain weighs just 3 pounds and has 100 billion cells!

FREE SOLO!

Alex Honnold (1985-) is the world's greatest free solo mountain climber. To free solo means to scale mountains without ropes, harnesses, or any safety equipment. In 2008, he became the first to scale the face of Half Dome, the majestic granite formation in Yosemite National Park, California. Neuroscientists were curious as to whether Honnald's brain, specifically his amygdala, is wired differently from other brains. In 2016, Alex participated in a fMRI study where he was shown 200 photographic images that would incite fear in most individuals. How did Alex's amygdala respond? The test results showed very little activity in his amygdala. Scientists don't have the advantage of being able to go back to when Alex first started climbing to study his brain, but the consensus is that, as a free solo climber, Alex has gradually built up his ability to conquer his fears. His visualization of each climb and his increase in confidence and competence has Alex feeling less anxious about each progressively difficult endeavor. Check out this video to learn more.

Honnold brain

Now your brain has two pieces of information to process. The sight of the person coming toward you and the sound of that person's voice as they greet you. The occipital and temporal lobes work together to identify the person walking toward you. Other sections of the brain collaborate to help figure out whether you know this person or whether it's a stranger.

Finally, your frontal lobe kicks in! This is where decision-making happens—your brain helps you decide and recognize whether this person is a friend or foe or just a stranger.

What else might help your decision? Your sense of smell? As the person gets closer, their particular scent reaches your olfactory bulbs located deep in your brain in the limbic system. Your sense of smell helps you determine if the person is your friend. Your brain then sends signals to the muscles in your hand to reach out and fist bump your friend. In real time, this whole process occurs in under a second!

BEHAVIOR CENTERS

The limbic system is a rich place in your brain. It's the area that governs emotion and memory. Scientists don't always agree which brain structures are included in the limbic system, but in this book, we'll take a look at the amygdala, the hypothalamus, and the hippocampus.

Let's start with the amygdala. The term comes from the Latin word for "almond." In fact, the amygdala looks like two almonds sitting side by side. Can you remember a situation when you felt fear? That was your amygdala at work. The amygdala is the part of your brain that regulates and perceives fear. But what if you were the person inspiring fear in someone else? Have you ever acted as a bully? That aggression stems from the amygdala, too.

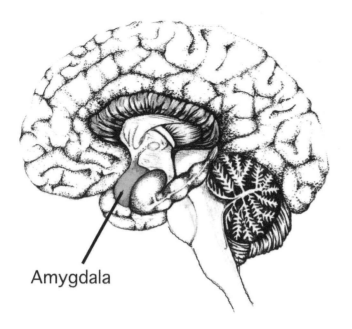

Amygdala

In scientific experiments involving brain scans of the amygdala in humans, when people were shown pictures that provoked anger, the amygdala fired up. And when scientists placed an electrode on a subject's amygdala and stimulated it, the amygdala produced rage. Scientists were able to prove that the amygdala is involved when you feel angry. Scientists have also found connections between the anxiety you feel, such as when taking a test, and the amygdala.

Have you ever done something just because everyone else did? This is known as conformity. The amygdala is the section of the brain that houses the ability to separate from the crowd. But the amygdala doesn't work by itself. As we've seen before, different parts of the brain work together to accomplish certain emotions and actions.

The amygdala seems to function by setting off alarms to other parts of the brain and body.

The word *hippocampus* comes from the Greek word meaning "sea horse" or "sea monster." The hippocampus has a shape similar to a seahorse!

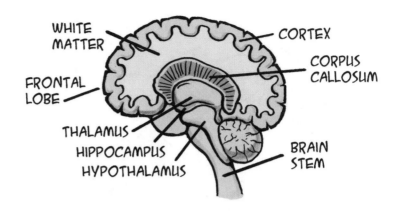

WHITE MATTER

CORTEX

FRONTAL LOBE

CORPUS CALLOSUM

THALAMUS

HIPPOCAMPUS

HYPOTHALAMUS

BRAIN STEM

PSYCH!

Many emotions are processed in the limbic system.

When you experience stress, the amygdala sends an alarm to the hypothalamus. The hypothalamus is like a command center. It signals the pituitary gland to produce a certain hormone, which in turn signals the adrenal glands, located above the kidneys, to increase the production of a hormone called cortisol, also known as the stress hormone.

The hypothalamus serves a role in our bodies similar to a school administrator at school, the center of communication that both receives messages and ensures proper delivery of messages. It makes decisions through the endocrine system, a group of glands that produce hormones that regulate many processes in our bodies.

The main role of the hypothalamus is to keep the body in a constant state of homeostasis, or balance, through the production and regulation of the body's hormones.

What did you have for breakfast this morning? What's your favorite holiday memory? You can't answer these questions without a hippocampus! If the hippocampus is damaged as a result of an illness, such as Alzheimer's disease, or in an accident, a person can experience both loss of memory and the inability to make new long-term memories. They might not be able to remember something that happened yesterday as a result of the damage, but could remember events from the distant past, since long-term memories are stored elsewhere.

The most interesting part of the brain as it relates to your behavior is the frontal lobe. The frontal lobe is the boss of your brain. This section has good organizational skills, including categorizing what you learn and then starting an action based on an executive decision and delayed gratification. The frontal lobe is awesome at long-term planning. It also helps reel in the emotions and is a watchdog for impulsive actions.

AUTOMATIC VS. CONTROLLED PROCESSING

Does the brain process information automatically or do we have to think about our actions? Psychologist John Stroop (1897–1973) studied reaction times in humans as part of his research. In 1929, he created a simple test to record reaction times that would go on to be known as a Stroop test. Little did he know that his test and the paper he produced describing his results would become one of the most well-known studies in the field of psychology.

The Stroop test (and what is now known as the Stroop effect, the name given to the results of the test) demonstrates something important. The brain processes what seems to be conflicting information differently from how it processes information that seems to be simple and straightforward. Sound confusing? Let's look more closely.

One common way to demonstrate the Stroop effect is to have someone read aloud the colors of a series of words. The trick is, the words themselves name a different color from the color of the letters. Your brain uses different areas to process color and words, and those two processes struggle when you try to name the color of the words correctly.

LEAPING TO JUDGMENT

Recent studies have demonstrated that automatic processing and decision-making involve gathering information from someone's facial expressions. The research shows that our automatic mind forms impressions of someone based on whether they are smiling at us or appear indifferent. Through our automatic processing, we make judgments about a person. Of course, people have bad days. Perhaps a person's typical, happy demeanor isn't present, and we've made a judgment in error, based on what our automatic mind perceives. Through controlled processing, we can intentionally greet the other person in a way that doesn't reflect our automatic thinking. We might even make a difference in someone's mood by being friendly when greeted with a scowl.

Give the Stroop test a try—
do you find yourself
stumbling as you name the
colors of the words? You
will need a keyboard to
take this test.

 Stroop test

RED	YELLOW
BLUE	**PURPLE**
GREEN	**BLACK**

The Stroop test shows that our behavior is often controlled by unconscious thought.

"HEY, YOU!"

Another example of unconscious thought is a noisy cafeteria, where you might be having a conversation with a friend and are suddenly distracted by someone shouting your name from across the room. Above all that extra noise, it's easy to hear your own name. At any given moment, the mind is processing information without conscious effort. This information causes people to behave in certain ways.

We might like to believe our actions are always a product of informed decisions, but research shows that this is not the case. Many of our decisions are generated without much conscious contemplation.

Do you ride the school bus every day? Same route, same time? Do you ever arrive at the school wondering how you got there, not remembering anything about the trip? This is an example of unconscious thought taking over.

This happens because the mind is made of two systems that process information from our environment. These are the controlled system and the automatic system. The controlled system is just as the term suggests—that actions are intentional.

Learning to ride a bike involves controlled processing. You have to think about how to get on the bike, where the pedals are, where the brakes are, and how to stay balanced. When you are first learning to ride a bike, you have to consciously think about what you are doing while riding it. Once you've learned, however, many of your actions on the bike are automatic.

The automatic system is similar to being on autopilot. Take eating a bowl of soup, for example. You don't consciously think about picking up the spoon, dipping it into the bowl, scooping up some soup, lifting the spoon to your mouth, and then sipping the soup. All those actions just happen automatically. You've learned how to perform the series of steps in the past and automatically do them.

The difference between automatic behavior and controlled, desired behavior stems from different mental abilities and processes, including visual cues, memory, problem-solving, and decision-making.

As we learned earlier, the prefrontal cortex is not fully developed until you are in your mid-20s. What does that mean for your brain and your behavior in your teens? We'll explore that in the next chapter.

PSYCH!
\\\\\\\\\\\\\\\\\\\\\\\\\

Delayed gratification means being able to save a reward for later instead of choosing to be rewarded immediately. Imagine saving money at the bank. Sure, you could take all your money and spend it, but if you practice delayed gratification and save it, the money will be there when you need it.

KEY QUESTIONS

- **What are the three main sections of your brain? What is the function of each?**
- **What are some of the roles of the amygdala in your behavior?**
- **What are some of the differences between automatic thought and controlled thought? Why do we need both to function?**

TEXT TO WORLD

What thoughts or actions have you performed so often they come to you automatically?

MODEL NEURON AND SYNAPSE BEHAVIOR

Scientists use models to help them understand and explain complex concepts. Models are especially important when studying processes that aren't easily seen—such as those that happen within the brain! In this activity, you and a group of friends will model the behavior of a neuron. Take a look at the neuron on page 13. How can you and your friends create the same image using just your bodies?

- **Each person holds a penny in their right hand and positions themselves so you all form a model of a neuron.** Create a neuron chain by forming a line, with each person standing next to each other at arms' length.

- **Imitate the input of a sensory message by having the first student in the line give their penny to the person next to them, without touching!** Continue to pass sensory messages down the neuron chain by passing the growing collection of pennies to the next person. How does this model the behavior of a synapse?

- **In an actual neuron, what would happen when the last person had the entire collection of pennies?** What does this mean for the imaginary muscle that receives that information?

> To investigate more, find out if anyone dropped their pennies. What does this demonstrate about synapses? What does it show about interruptions in the passage of information through neurons?

VOCAB LAB

Write down what you think each word means. What root words can you find to help you? What does the context of the word tell you?

action potential, amygdala, cerebrum, hippocampus, neuron, neurotransmitter, prefrontal cortex, and **synapse**.

Compare your definitions with those of your friends or classmates. Did you all come up with the same meanings? Turn to the text and glossary if you need help.

Chapter 2 ▶
The Teenage Brain

The teenage brain is the same size as an adult brain, but the adult brain processes information and makes decisions very differently. Partly this is because of the physical development of the brain, and partly it's because teenagers haven't yet had certain learning opportunities and experiences.

The brain is at the core of what we do, think, and say, but that doesn't mean scientists understand everything about it. In fact, scientists are still working hard to solve the mysteries of this amazing organ. And many of those scientists are paying careful attention to the teenage brain. Why? Because so much is happening in the teen brain in terms of development. It's a fascinating time of change.

It's not that younger brains aren't fully grown—a teenage brain is just as large as an adult brain. In fact, the teenage brain has a greater capacity to learn than an adult's brain—that's basically the main job of teenagers. Their brains are working overtime to accommodate all that they are discovering.

But interestingly, the brain develops from the back to the front. Early on in our lives, the brain develops in essential areas that control vision, hearing, balance, and touch.

The limbic system, the emotional center of the brain, develops next. However, the front part of the brain, the prefrontal cortex, is the last to fully develop. And that's the part that controls the rest.

The teenage brain has an amazing ability to process and store information. Let's break this all down and assemble that teen brain puzzle a bit more and discover its role in teen behavior.

GRAY MATTER AND WHITE MATTER

The brain is made up of all the areas we covered in Chapter 1, but it also consists of gray matter and white matter. If you held an actual human brain in your hand, it would be about the size of your two fists and feel like squishy pasta. And the brain kind of looks like squishy pasta, too, except it's grayish in color.

The outside of the brain looks wrinkly. The grooves that make these wrinkles are called sulci and the ridges are called gyri.

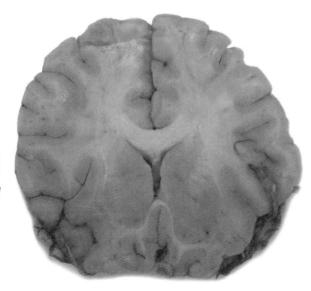

A cross section of a human brain

credit: *World Journal of Surgical Oncology* 2006 (CC BY 2.0)

If you look at a cross-section of the brain, you'll see the gray matter on the perimeter of the brain. The gray matter is home to neuron cell bodies and glial cells, which provide nutrients and energy to neurons.

To understand the physiological difference between gray matter and white matter, it helps to know that gray matter is the area of the brain where commands are initiated. The white matter is the area where the information is carried from place to place through those axons covered in myelin.

Remember how neurons connect with one another to help the brain control our bodies and behavior? Remember the axon on the neuron? It's the path where messages travel from the cell body of a neuron to the axon terminals. The neuron then sends its message through neurotransmitters to the synapses to other neurons. And so on.

Neurons connect to other neurons close by. To connect to neurons in other parts of the brain, the neurons send processes through the white matter of the brain and then along the spinal cord to activate muscles and nerves in our body.

> The white matter of the brain is called that because of its color—in reality and on MRI scans, the color of these parts of the brain is whitish.

The myelin that covers the neurons in the white matter is white. The myelin acts as a fatty insulator that makes the electrical signals move more freely and quickly. Have you seen electrical wires coated in plastic insulation so the electrical charge stays the course and does its work? Myelin works in just the same way.

DISAPPEARING GRAY MATTER?

One fascinating fact about the teenage brain is that, at the start of adolescence, teenagers have a greater volume of gray matter and more synapses than adults. As a young person goes through their teen years, the volume of gray matter is reduced as synaptic connections that aren't used are pruned away. Plus, myelination increases. Remember, the connections that are made again and again become strong, while those that aren't made very often eventually disappear.

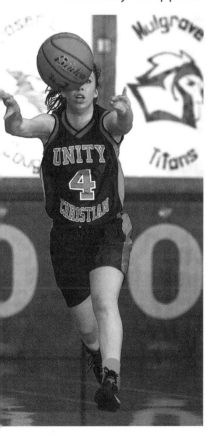

The neurons in a teenage brain get pruned as a young person learns from their experiences. Your brain doesn't become smaller, it becomes more efficient.

Are you a basketball player? How many shots do you take every day? The more you square yourself up to the basket, bend from the knees to use your lower body strength, pump the ball up into the air, and let the ball spin off of your fingertips toward the basket, the more your brain remembers the action in unison with your body. This is true in any sport, dance, puzzle, game, or scene from a play.

MORE ABOUT MYELIN

When you are an infant, myelination occurs at a rapid pace. This process corresponds with motor development, including crawling and walking. This quicker communication helps the progress of communication from other parts of the brain to the prefrontal cortex. Have you ever done a tune-up of your bicycle or skateboard? Did you grease the chain or the wheels? What did it feel like afterward? Pretty smooth ride! In your white matter, as the myelin forms around the axons in the neurons in your brain, the electrical impulses move faster and more smoothly. As a result, the activity in different parts of your prefrontal cortex becomes more coordinated with the rest of your brain.

Recent scientific studies show that although the volume of gray matter in a teenage brain is decreasing due to synapses being pruned and the myelination of neurons, the density of the gray matter is becoming greater. Studies have also shown that although female brains are lower in volume due to their smaller size, the gray matter is thicker than a male's brain. This explains why cognitive ability in females and males is similar.

For hundreds of years, however, society rated female intelligence as lower than that of males. Many used this as an excuse for gender discrimination.

THE WIRING DEVELOPMENT OF YOUR BRAIN

As you've learned, the brain develops from the back of the brain to the top front. Think of the construction of a house. Where do builders begin? It doesn't make sense to start in the attic, right?

When a house is being built, the wiring starts at the bottom of the structure, the basement, and is fed up to the top floors. In the brain, the process of axons becoming myelinated starts from the back of the brain and works up toward the front at the top.

As a result of this pattern, the last area in your brain to mature is your prefrontal cortex. Remember, this is the area involved in decision-making, planning, and self-control.

It's not that you don't have the capabilities in your prefrontal cortex to make decisions, plan ahead, or be more in control of your emotions.

It's just that the signals to help you with these processes aren't developing fast enough to control the overriding emotions. Let's take a closer look at the relationship between how you act and your prefrontal cortex.

COGNITIVE DEVELOPMENT

What is the relationship between the development of your prefrontal cortex and your behavior? To answer this question, let's take a look at cognitive development.

Cognitive development is the ability to think and reason. As people grow and mature, they form new ideas and questions and can consider many different points of view. One huge step in cognitive development that comes in the teen years is developing the ability to think about the process of thinking!

credit: U.S. Air Force photo by Airman 1st Class Shawna L. Keyes

WHO'S TO BLAME FOR ADOLESCENCE?

Granville Stanley Hall (1846–1924) was a pioneer in the field of psychology. Dr. Hall was the first American to obtain a Ph.D., a postgraduate doctoral degree, in psychology. Dr. Hall dedicated a lot of his time to studying adolescent development, particularly in the area of adolescent aggression. He established adolescence as a chapter in human development. Dr. Hall is known as the "father of adolescence" due to his work in this important point in development. He defined your age and stage in the world of psychology!

Three renowned neurology experts offer insights into the teenage brain and what you can do to take care of yours. What advice is given to adolescents? Why is this important?

 Franklin Institute growing up

Have you had discussions with adults about differing opinions on a topic? Do you spend any time contemplating what is going on in your own mind? These are signs of cognitive development. It's the process of becoming more self-aware than you were when you were younger.

Even as a teenager's cognition develops beyond childhood, cognitive choices and behaviors can be impacted because the prefrontal cortex isn't fully developed. Some teens are terrific at applying logic to schoolwork, but struggle to do the same in their personal lives. Have you ever stayed up all night finishing a report because you put off doing it earlier? Could you maybe have planned your time better? Or, maybe you worked hard to finish the paper, but you then spent too much time afterward playing a video game and forgot to get your gear together for football practice and ran out of the house without your cleats?

Just because your brain is still changing and growing, that's not a pass for misbehavior or poor choices. As a teen, you're capable of making good decisions, as guided by the adults in your life.

> Teens are still accountable for their actions and decisions.

RISK-TAKING

One of the most important roles the still-developing prefrontal cortex plays in your behavior involves risk-taking. By examining teen brains during an fMRI, scientists have discovered teenagers' brains don't "fire up" their prefrontal cortex during risky decision-making. The less brain activity taking place in the prefrontal cortex, the poorer the risk assessment.

Teens simply don't have the best ability to judge the riskiness of a situation, because their brains aren't physically able to do so yet.

However, scientists are learning that in some areas, teens are just as good at risk assessment as adults. So, what's the difference?

The answers to those questions are found in the greater roles that friends and peers have in the lives of teenagers, and the different effects of dopamine on a teenager's brain vs. an adult's brain.

Middle school and high school are great times to make friends. Some of those friends might last the rest of your life! And teens tend to care about what their friends think. Friends and peers have a huge impact on most teens when they make decisions, both good and bad.

STRATEGIZE!

Even though their prefrontal cortex isn't fully formed, teenagers are still expected to be organized, do well in school, and even hold down a job. Here are some steps you can take to make sure you're on top of things:

• Make lists of tasks

• Change a big, overwhelming task into smaller tasks by breaking the big one down into steps

• Use a calendar to organize deadlines

• Pack your backpack for the next day before you go to bed

• Think twice before you do something. Ask yourself, "Will this action hurt me or someone I love?"

Check out this video from National Geographic Brain Games demonstrating teen risk-taking behavior when peers are present. Do you think your driving behavior would change when friends are with you?

 Brain Games teenage brain

ARVID CARLSSON

Arvid Carlsson (1923–2018) was a scientist from Sweden who discovered the role of the neurotransmitter dopamine in Parkinson's disease, a disorder of the central nervous system that affects movements, often resulting in tremors. Dr. Carlsson developed a way to measure dopamine in the brain and learned the greatest concentrations were in the basal ganglia, deep within the brain. Through his studies, he ultimately discovered a treatment to help patients with Parkinson's. For his work, he received the Nobel Prize in Physiology and Medicine in 2000.

Have you ever been offered a cigarette or a beer? Did you feel free to say no or pressured to say yes? There's a high likelihood your decision was influenced by the people around you.

Peers play a greater role in your life during adolescence than they did in childhood. Young children aren't that concerned about what people think of them. Have you ever seen little kids dancing away in the middle of a restaurant? They aren't worrying about being judged. But, as we get older, we become more self-conscious and concerned about what others, especially peers, think. There's brain science behind this phenomenon.

Scientists have studied the brain activity of adolescents who believed they were being watched. Viewed through an fMRI, teenagers' prefrontal cortexes became much more active when they thought about other people watching them. This reaction signaled anxiety. When teens had an audience, they were very aware of it.

> Scientists have learned through these studies that the prefrontal cortexes of teens respond to social situations more so than any other age group.

The experiments prove that teens think about themselves more than other age groups. Social situations are more significant. They carry a lot of emotional weight, resulting in a lot of self-conscious stress response.

Think about the last school dance you went to. Did you hold off on dancing until a lot of other friends were out on the floor?

This brain is being studied with fMRI.

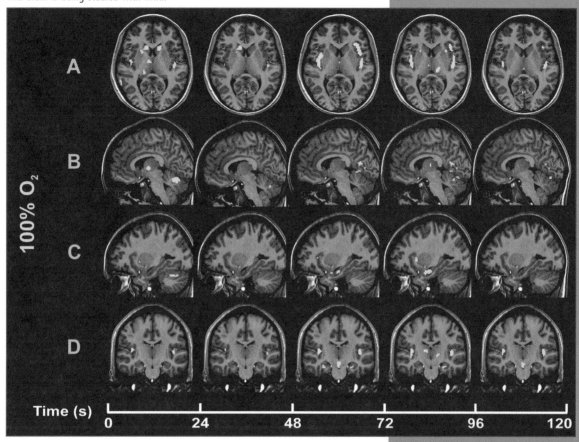

Or, maybe you love dancing at home when no one is watching, but when there are others around, you don't venture out onto the dance floor. This happens because most teens care a lot about what other people think of them. Their brains make them more sensitive than adults to the reward of peer relationships.

The teenage brain is also in search of something besides peer approval—excitement! Why? Because of a neurotransmitter known as dopamine.

The neurotransmitter dopamine is complex and has many functions. It is involved in memory, physical movement, and the process of rewarding experiences. Learn more about dopamine in this video. Where is dopamine found in your brain?

2 minute neuro dopamine

REWARD CENTERS IN THE BRAIN

Dopamine plays an important role in things we do daily. It is involved in how we move, as well as what we eat, how we learn, and even whether or not addiction is a part of our lives.

Remember, neurotransmitters act as messengers between brain cells. Different neurotransmitters are made in different parts of the brain. Two main brain areas produce dopamine. One, called the substantia nigra, sits near the base of your brain. Another area that makes dopamine is the ventral tegmental area (VTA), located in the mid-brain, adjacent to the substantia nigra.

The term *substantia nigra* means "black substance" in Latin and refers to the dark color of this tiny strip of tissue.

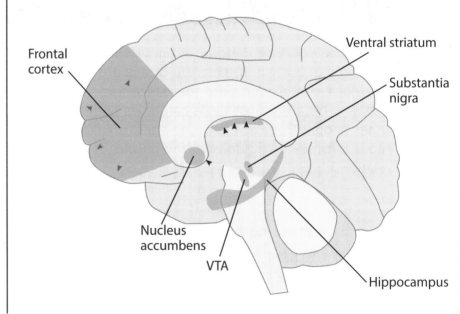

Frontal cortex

Ventral striatum

Substantia nigra

Nucleus accumbens

VTA

Hippocampus

The dopamine produced by these two areas relays signals that travel throughout the brain. Dopamine from the substantia nigra helps voluntary movements and speech. Dopamine from the VTA does something entirely different—the dopamine is released into the brain when you expect to receive or actually receive a reward.

One area of the brain that receives the input of dopamine is the ventral striatum. The ventral striatum is closely associated with decision-making, risk, and reward. Dopamine is its most vital neurotransmitter—thoughts of gain, whether that's money or recognition, will increase dopamine in the nucleus accumbens area of the ventral striatum, while thoughts of loss decrease dopamine.

When was the last time you felt rewarded for a certain behavior? Did you get a good grade, praise for helping the family, or a ribbon in an art show? What did it feel like? Those good feelings were caused by the dopamine being released in your brain as you got your reward. This dopamine release tells the brain that whatever it just experienced is worth getting more of.

> Your brain tells you it wants more,
> so you work toward making the
> right decisions to feed the reward
> or pleasure centers in your brain.

Do you ever feel the need to do something that feels rewarding again and again? Maybe you helped a neighbor and they paid you $10 for your work. Those $10 make you want to help her again, right? Dopamine helps reinforce positive actions so we want to do them again.

THE MARSHMALLOW TEST

In the 1960s, a famous experiment called the Marshmallow Test was created. Preschool children were given a choice between one reward—a marshmallow—that they could eat right away, and a larger reward—two marshmallows—that they would have to wait up to 20 minutes longer to earn. The study provided interesting information on instant gratification. The scientists kept studying those who participated in the experiment. What they discovered was that if children were able to wait for the larger reward, they were more successful later in life than those who couldn't wait. However, a more recent study found that being able to delay gratification doesn't necessarily lead to better outcomes in life. Instead, a subject's background, home environment, and caretakers have a greater impact on a child's outcome in life.

Check out this video of young children trying to resist temptation. How long do you think they waited for the reward? Would you wait?

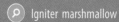 Igniter marshmallow

PSYCH!

Dr. Frances E. Jensen, the department chair of neurology at the University of Pennsylvania and the author of *The Teenage Brain*, states that if the human brain is a puzzle, the teenage brain is a puzzle waiting to be completed. She is an internationally known expert in neurology and teenage behavior and a mother to two sons.

Since friends and peers and acceptance mean more to teens than any other age group, they make decisions based on that acceptance. When you do something and your peers approve, dopamine is released, you feel good, and you want to do it again.

Reward and reinforcement help us learn where to find important things such as food or water, so that we can go back for more. Reward and reinforcement created by dopamine have a downside, too. The drugs cocaine, nicotine, and heroin cause huge boosts in dopamine. The high that people feel when they use drugs comes partly from that dopamine burst. As a result, it causes people to want to use those drugs again and again—even though they are harmful. The brain wants more and more of this feeling, so it craves more and more drugs. This can lead to drug abuse and, eventually, addiction.

HORMONES

Has anyone every blamed your behavior on your hormones? Teenagers have surging hormones, which affect behavior in many ways.

Do you feel tired when you get up to go to school? Some teenagers have a lot of trouble falling asleep at night and even more trouble getting up in the morning. Hormones are involved in the regulation of day and night rhythms, and these hormones encourage teenagers to start feeling sleepy much later at the night than adults or children. Add the early morning school schedule to the mix and you've got tired teenagers.

Hormones can also affect emotions. Scientists at the University of British Columbia are conducting a study on how the sex hormones estrogen and testosterone shape teenagers' emotions.

The main purpose is to investigate how the significant changes in hormone levels in teens affect their emotions, interactions with family and peers, and overall mental health. The scientists hope that the study will provide insights for teenagers and their caregivers as to how hormones impact their social and emotional development.

Recently, scientists have discovered that receptors for hormones exist in many areas of the body, including the brain.

Other hormones influence your brain development, and, ultimately, your behavior. One of those is oxytocin, which is involved in the bonding that happens in relationships. Women in general have higher levels of oxytocin, which is released in the brain when a person touches or even looks at someone they love.

Teenage brains are doing amazing things. Knowing that your behavior stems from the activity in your head can help you decipher events and relationships and keep you thriving.

While the brain has plenty to do with how people act, there are other players in the game—in the next chapter, we'll look at genetics and the environment!

Check out this time-lapse video of neurons firing!

 neuron time lapse video

KEY QUESTIONS

- **What are some of the differences between teen brains and adult brains?**
- **Why are friends and peers more important to teens than to young children?**

TEXT TO WORLD

What are some ways you see teens behaving differently from adults and younger children?

CHOICES AND CONSEQUENCES

Risk-taking behavior can offer learning opportunities! And not all risk-taking leads to bad outcomes. Taking risks can fall into categories of risk, all affecting you in different ways. Take a look.

VOCAB LAB

Write down what you think each word means. What root words can you find to help you? What does the context of the word tell you?

adolescence, cognitive, dopamine, gray matter, myelin, and **testosterone.**

Compare your definitions with those of your friends or classmates. Did you all come up with the same meanings? Turn to the text and glossary if you need help.

- **In your classroom or with a group of friends, pair up in twos and discuss the following risk-taking activities.** Do you consider these positive risks or negative ones? Make notes on which kind of risk is involved in each of the choices.

Risk-Taking Activities	Positive	Negative	Types of Risk				
			Social	Physical	Legal	Financial	Psychological
Auditioning for the school play							
Rock climbing at the gym							
Jumping off the high dive							
Smoking a cigarette							
Driving over the speed limit							
Speaking out on behalf of a friend							
Lying to your parents							
Telling a friend's secret to another person							
Stealing a magazine from the store							
Skipping school							

- **Once you've completed the activity, discuss with the group as a whole.** Did each pair find several categories of risk for different activities?

- **Are there ever benefits to taking risks?** Why or why not?

To investigate more, discuss what are unacceptable risks to you and your friends. What type of consequences might there be for different risks?

Chapter 3 ▶
Genes, Environment, and Behavior

Which has more impact on someone's behavior—their genes or their environment?

Human behavior is an incredibly complex process that is influenced by many, many different factors, both genetic ones and environmental ones. The debate over which has more impact is ongoing!

Have you ever heard the phrase "nature vs. nurture?" This phrase stems from an age-old scientific debate. Some people believe that genes have more influence on who we are and how we behave. They think genetics, or nature, not only determine what we look like, but also determine our personality and how we behave. Those in the nurture camp believe that environmental factors, including early childhood influences and experiences, friendships, and surrounding culture, such as school, are larger factors than our genetic makeup when it comes to the type of people we grow up to be.

Consider star soccer players who never seem to miss a shot. How did they get so good at soccer? Is it because their parents are also great athletes? That's nature at work. But maybe they are so good because they practice for an hour every day. That's an example of nurture.

It's likely that both nature and nurture have a lot to do with someone's ability to play a sport well.

What about the students in school who are always first to raise their hands and nail the answer every time? Are they smart because both of their parents are college professors? Or is it because they spend hours in the library every week? Which of these is an example of nature and which is nurture? Finally, how about the bully? Do bullies act the way they do because their ancestors behaved the same way a hundred years ago? Or is it because they have witnessed this kind of behavior in their home?

The nature vs. nurture debate has no easy answers. Let's take a look at some of the work done around this question.

CELLS: THE FOUNDATION

Cells are the basic units of every human being. We have trillions of cells in our bodies! Human cells are eukaryotic, which means they include a nucleus surrounded by a membrane that houses genetic material. The structures that hold the genetic material are called chromosomes. The genetic material within chromosomes is called chromatin.

PSYCH!
\\\\\\\\\\\\\\\\\\\

Francis Galton (1822–1911) wore many hats in his life. He was an explorer, anthropologist, and psychologist from Britain. He created the term "nature vs. nature."

A cell and some of its structures

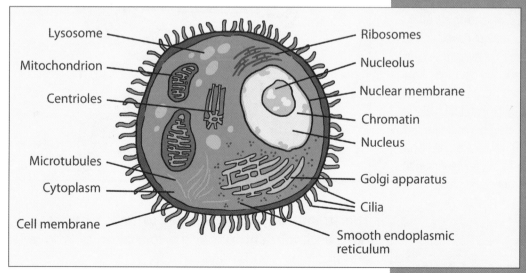

Lysosome

Mitochondrion

Centrioles

Microtubules

Cytoplasm

Cell membrane

Ribosomes

Nucleolus

Nuclear membrane

Chromatin

Nucleus

Golgi apparatus

Cilia

Smooth endoplasmic reticulum

Most humans have 22 pairs of matching chromosomes. The remaining pair contains the sex chromosomes, either XY chromosomes for boys or XX chromosomes for girls.

CAREER: CHILD PSYCHOLOGISTS

Child psychologists study, analyze, and diagnose the mental, social, and emotional development of children of all ages, from birth through the teen years. Child psychologists study many areas of development and behavior, including genetics, the brain, how children mature, and social and environmental factors. A child psychologist will help treat a child who is facing developmental issues and challenges.

Most humans have 46 chromosomes. Each chromosome consists of tight coils of a single chromatin fiber, called a nucleosome. Inside a nucleosome, we see the telltale double strand of deoxyribonucleic acid (DNA) wrapped around protein bodies called histones. Histones squish the DNA into the compact structure of the nucleus.

DNA is twisted in a shape called a double helix. If you straightened out the strands of DNA, it would look like a ladder. The rungs of the ladder are made up of units of four bases—adenine, cytosine, guanine, and thymine, or A, C, G, T.

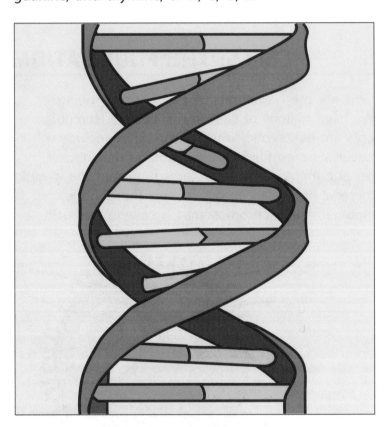

The strands of DNA have rules to their patterns and have an important role in the formation of who you are and how you behave.

The four bases on DNA (A, C, G and T), along with a five-sided sugar and a phosphate group, create the basic building block of DNA, called nucleotides. But there are certain rules as to what can play together in the genetic sandbox. A (adenine) pairs only with T (thymine) and C (cytosine) and G (guanine) always bond together.

These nucleotides and the sequence they are in are responsible for making important proteins. These proteins trigger various biological actions to carry out both important life functions, such as breathing, and elements of behavior. The stretch of nucleotides that "codes" these actions is called a gene.

WHAT IS A GENE?

A gene is the basic unit of heredity. Every person has two copies of each gene, one inherited from each parent. Genes are why you have the eye color, hair color, and type of skin that you do.

DNA is like the architect of your body. It carries the instructions needed to build and maintain the many different cells that make you who you are. All of the instructions carried by DNA are called a genome.

Humans are very similar as a group in their DNA. Your genome is 99 percent the same as the person sitting next to you. That remaining 1 percent is why you are unique. Your genome not only affects what you look like, but it also determines your risk for disease and other things, such as whether you are predisposed to becoming addicted to alcohol or drugs.

Scientists who study behavior genetics also believe your genes are involved in how you act.

This video offers insights into cells, DNA, chromosomes, and genes. What do genes determine?

 SciTech guru genes DNA

HGP

The Human Genome Project was an international project that set out to map all the genes of humans. The main goals of the project were defined in 1988 and the full sequence was completed in April 2003. The international effort to map the 3 billion DNA letters in the human genome is considered one of the greatest undertakings in the world of science. The results were released to scientists around the world, allowing them to further their studies in areas such as identification of human gene diseases. In 1990, when the study began, scientists had discovered only 100 human gene diseases. Now, more than 1,400 have been discovered.

Why is DNA Sequencing Important?

The impacts of understanding the DNA sequencing of the human genome include both the discovery and treatment of diseases. Previously, it might take years for a pediatrician to identify a rare genetic disease in a child. Now, through a genome study of the family, a diagnosis can be determined much sooner. By sequencing cancer genomes, scientists are discovering which drugs specifically work on which cancer cells, offering targeted treatment for patients.

To help understand the significance of genes, think of them as the conductor of a train. Just as a conductor controls the direction in which a train travels, a gene specifies the production of a specific type of protein. The gene has to be activated for the protein to be produced (the train goes) and deactivated to stop producing it (the train stops). Genes come with an on/off switch, much as a train engine does.

Every cell in your body has genes that work this way. As you grew and developed, the stop/go feature helped determine which genes formed the shape of your nose to make it more like your mom's or more like your dad's.

Hormones and environmental inputs are part of the process, too, as they are involved in turning switches off and on for particular genes. The study of this impact of hormones and the environment on our genes is called epigenetics.

EPIGENETICS

Epigenetics is the study of biological mechanisms that switch genes on and off during an organism's lifetime. Scientists who study epigenetics look at many different factors—what you eat, when you sleep, how you exercise and age, plus how the behaviors of your ancestors might impact you.

What were your grandparents' habits like? Did one of them smoke? Did one of them run long distances? Believe it or not, their decisions might affect whether certain genes in your body are activated. In a family member with an addiction such as smoking, healthy genes could be suppressed and cancerous genes activated. Those genes could be passed down to you in some form.

If a family member exercises regularly, you might reap the benefits of their healthy choices.

Of course, your own decisions about how you live your life are the main source of the quality of your life, but it's interesting to trace possible links between yourself and your ancestors. The study of epigenetics is helping to discover our uniqueness— why you enjoy certain foods and beverages, why your hair color is what it is, and whether you are sociable or not.

Scientists might someday make great inroads into eliminating genetic diseases by learning how to turn certain genes off and on.

SOCIAL GENES

Are your friends like you? Do they look like you? Do you act alike? How could that be?

PSYCH!
\\\\\\\\\\\\\\\\\\

The Human Genome Project estimates that the human body contains between 20,000 and 25,000 genes.

Are these friends genetically similar? They might be!

Have you ever heard the phrase "birds of a feather flock together"? This means that those who are like one another will be attracted to one another.

PSYCH!

\\\\\\\\\\\\\\\\\\\\\\\\\\

The term "homophily" comes from a Greek word meaning "together" and "friendship."

Scientists have determined that humans tend to form social relationships with others who resemble them. We make friends with people who are like us. But why is that? Is it because people who are similar often live near each other and join many of the same groups? Is it because we select friends who share characteristics with us? Do genes help dictate who we are friends with?

A study was conducted in 2018 to explore the role that genes play in social relationships. Scientists studied a sample of more than 5,000 American adolescents, comparing their genomes with friends and strangers to see if there were similarities. The researchers compared traits such as height, body mass index, grades, and educational accomplishments.

They discovered that pairs of friends were more genetically similar than pairs of random people. However, they weren't nearly as alike as siblings.

Plus, the similarities were strongest when certain traits were considered. Participants were more likely to be similar in terms of body mass index and academic success, for example, than height.

Why are friends more genetically similar to one another than they are to randomly selected peers? The scientists considered two hypotheses. The first is that friends are more genetically alike because they tend to choose friends who have similar physical characteristics, such as being short or tall. Friends are often similar as far as education levels in family, too. This process of choosing friends is called social homophily.

The other hypothesis is that friends are genetically similar because people tend to form friendships within their environments. For example, we tend to form friendships with people who live in the same neighborhood or who go to the same school. Scientists refer to this process as social structuring. When genetics influence the environments people live in, this can result in friends having similar genes.

The scientists also found evidence of what is known as the "social-genetic effect." Their findings suggest that the genetics of friends and schoolmates influenced the students' education, even after accounting for each of the student's own genetics.

In other words, there is proof that you are, in part, who you are based on who you surround yourself with.

Other studies that were begun in the late 1970s revealed some interesting data about the nature vs. nurture debate. Let's look more closely at twins and what they can teach us about psychology.

IT'S TWINS!

Have you ever met a pair of identical twins? If so, you'll notice that they look very similar. Their hair is similar, their eyes are the same color, and they are close in height and weight. Some identical twins can even pass themselves off as each other.

Spend some time with identical twins and you'll probably notice that they behave in similar ways, too. Maybe they both have the same high-pitched laugh or both twist their hair when they are nervous.

NATURE VS. NURTURE

Twins and their behavior have been studied for a long time. In 1875, British researcher Sir Francis Galton (1822–1911) concluded that, as a result of his studies of 80 twins, nature beat nurture in the nature vs. nurture argument. In 1922, Walter Jablonski conducted the first classical twin study, measuring the size of eyes in identical and nonidentical twins and revealing inherited traits. In the 1980s, Thomas J. Bouchard Jr. (1937–), along with Nancy L. Segal (1951–), began studying identical twins raised in different environments. Their studies revealed that even when raised separately, identical twins are similar in personality, mannerisms, and interests.

Fraternal twins are known as dizygotic, or DZ, "di" meaning two.

Identical twins are so alike because they share the same genes. Their genetic makeup is 100 percent the same. Identical twins are known in the world of science as MZ, or monozygotic twins. "Mono" means one. They are formed when an egg is fertilized by a sperm and the egg separates, creating two separate, identical eggs.

Fraternal twins, however, are different from the very beginning. These kinds of twins are created when two different eggs in a woman's body are fertilized by two different sperm. They share half their genetic makeup, just as any other siblings do.

Scientists are interested in studying twins because of what they can learn in terms of behavioral genetics, which is the study of genetic influences on behavior—the nature side of the debate.

What if a pair of identical twins was separated at birth? Would their interests be the same? Would their behavior be the same?

That's exactly what a psychologist set out to determine, starting in the 1970s. Dr. Thomas J. Bouchard Jr. of the University of Minnesota began a study that involved more than 100 sets of twins or triplets, both identical and fraternal.

He wanted to learn about their intelligence, personalities, temperaments, extracurricular interests, and social attitudes. Participants in the study completed nearly 50 hours of medical and psychological testing.

> The results of the study suggest that even when identical twins were reared apart, they were still similar in their personalities and behaviors.

Dr. Bouchard states that even though naturalists and animal breeders know that other species inherit behavior traits, scientists are hesitant to recognize the role of genes in human behavior. The conclusions of his study note that intelligence level is strongly affected by genetic factors. The study also suggests that psychological traits are inherited and are less impacted by environment than most scientists believe.

In 1979, a student of Dr. Bouchard brought to his attention the case of identical twins Jim Springer and Jim Lewis. The two Jims were separated just four weeks after they were born and raised by two different families 25 miles away from each other. The first time they met was at age 39 years.

They had many similarities, both in physical traits as well as choices and behavior. Both had married and divorced women named Linda, then married women named Betty. They had both named their sons James Allen. They smoked heavily, bit their nails, had heart problems, and suffered from migraine headaches.

Dr. Bouchard went on to study more than 137 pairs of twins who had been reared apart. Through his work, the genetic influence on behavior has become widely accepted.

HERITABILITY

Heritability is a measure of how differences in people's genes explain the differences in their traits or behavior. In the case of animals, heritability is the variation in a trait from animal to animal. Dogs are a perfect example of how heritable traits in behavior have been bred and developed through time. Breeders encourage certain desired behavior traits through breeding to produce animals that are suited for different roles, such as sheepherding, service work, and protection.

But this kind of breeding is not an exact science. A highly motivated working dog might produce a lazy offspring. Careful breeding efforts don't always produce the desired results. This is due to the complex combination of both nature and nurture, genes and environment, that are work in behavior.

Studying twins takes place all over the world. The Swedish Twins Registry was begun in the 1960s and contains information on 85,000 pairs of identical and fraternal twins. This extensive registry supports at least 30 ongoing projects on topics that include aging, dementia, cancer, and heart disease.

Let's explore the other side of the nature vs nurture debate through the work of scientists who argue that the environment plays a huge role in who you are, who you become, and how you behave.

PSYCH!

Do you remember learning to be afraid of something? Was there ever a time you weren't afraid of something, but then a person or an experience taught you to be afraid? An example of this might be a fear of sharks. You wouldn't know that sharks could hurt until you saw the movie *Jaws*!

NURTURE

Behaviorism, also known as behavior psychology, takes the position that all behaviors are developed mainly because of the environment, not genetics. Behaviorists theorize that responses to environmental factors cause people to behave in certain ways.

Some believe that any person can be trained to do anything, regardless of inherited traits or abilities. All it takes is the right conditioning, such as practicing steps every day to become a stellar dancer.

One of Skinner's teaching boxes
credit: Silly rabbit (CC BY 3.0)

Dr. John Watson (1878–1958) conducted early, controversial studies on the subject of conditioning in 1920. In the experiment, Dr. Watson and graduate student Rosalie Rayner (1899–1935) presented a variety of items to a nine-month-old baby boy known as "Albert B," or more often, "Little Albert." The objects included a live monkey, a dog, and a rat. Little Albert seemed to accept the items and even enjoyed playing with the white rat.

Then, Dr. Watson presented the objects again, but made a loud noise by hitting a metal pipe with a hammer when the baby was exposed to the objects. How do you suppose the baby reacted? How might you react? Little Albert cried and shied away from the objects. Dr. Watson's conclusions were that the baby didn't fear the objects at first, but through conditioning, the baby grew afraid because he was being taught to respond this way.

Another behaviorist, Dr. Burrhus Frederic Skinner (1904–1990), better known as B.F. Skinner, is famous for his experiments with rats. Dr. Skinner created a metal box, which became known as the Skinner Box. Inside the box was a metal bar. Dr. Skinner placed a rat in the box. Every time the rat pressed on the metal bar, the rat received a food pellet. Dr. Skinner observed and recorded the rat's behavior and noted that, as time passed, the rat learned that whenever it pressed the bar, food appeared. The rat began to press the bar to get fed. The rat's behavior resulted in being rewarded with food.

Dr. Skinner concluded from these studies that animals are conditioned by the responses they receive from their actions and the environment. He came up with the term "operant conditioning" to reflect his belief that behavior is a two-way process. That an action, or behavior, has a consequence—a reward or a punishment.

Learn more about the Little Albert experiment in this video. How do you feel about the experiment? What are some other issues with the process, beyond cruelty?

 Little Albert video

LIMITS OF BEHAVIORISM

Many sciences evolve as people gain knowledge and insight. And although Dr. Skinner might have found some correlation between reward and behavior, further studies have shown that the relationship is more complex than previously supposed. Do you know anyone who has stayed in a bad relationship long after they understood it was hurting them? According to behaviorism, getting hurt would teach us to avoid certain people. But that's not always the case. As we sometimes see in bad relationships, human behavior doesn't always conform to the rules of behaviorism.

The behaviorism of the early twentieth century has fallen out of fashion, though scientific research is still being done on behavior.

NURTURE OVERCOMING NATURE

Is it possible to overcome genetic traits, such as alcoholism and other addictions, through nurturing? Maybe! According to a 2009 study, a family-based prevention program created to help teens avoid substance abuse was effective for a group of young teens with genetic risk factors for such choices.

The study involved researchers from the University of Georgia, the National Institute on Alcohol Abuse and Alcoholism, and the National Institute on Drug Abuse. For two-and-a-half years, 11-year-old children were enrolled in Strong African American Families (SAAF), a program focused on substance abuse and prevention of risky behavior. Some children in the SAAF group carried the gene 5-HTTLPR, which is suspected to be associated with alcohol craving and substance abuse.

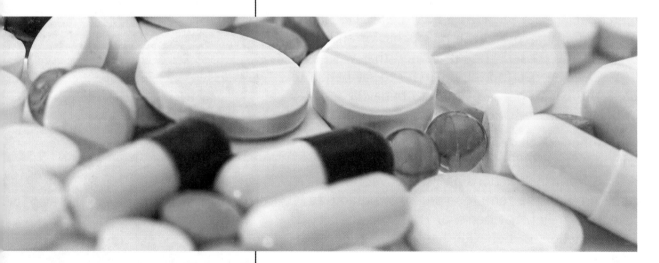

The program involved seven weeks of two-hour prevention sessions for both adults and children. The adults learned effective caregiving strategies, including monitoring and supporting their children, and the kids were taught how to set goals, deal with peer pressure, and avoid risk-taking activities.

The researchers found that the adolescents with the gene who participated in the program were no more likely than those without the gene to become involved in drinking, doing drugs, or being sexually active.

The results emphasized the importance of families and prevention programs in promoting healthy choices during adolescence, especially for children with genetic predisposition toward addiction.

Most experts believe that both nature and nurture impact our behavior. Scientists are finding that there is not one simple way to separate the variety of forces that impact behavior—both genetic factors and environmental factors, including home and social environments, and how they combine to impact behavior.

VOCAB LAB

Write down what you think each word means. What root words can you find to help you? What does the context of the word tell you?

behaviorism, ethics, heritability, predisposition, social homophily, and **social structuring.**

Compare your definitions with those of your friends or classmates. Did you all come up with the same meanings? Turn to the text and glossary if you need help.

KEY QUESTIONS

- Why are twins useful in studies that compare nature vs. nurture?
- How do theories change as scientists make discoveries? What does this tell us about scientific fact vs. opinion?
- Why should ethics be part of psychological experiments?

TEXT TO WORLD

Do you know a pair of twins? How are they different? How might their environment have caused these differences?

Ideas for Supplies ▼

- squishable fruit (banana, strawberry, or kiwi)
- sealable plastic bag
- water
- dish soap
- table salt
- coffee filter
- clear glasses (or test tubes)
- ice-cold rubbing alcohol (70 percent or higher)
- chopstick, toothpick, or paperclip

> To investigate more, try this experiment using other fruit. Is it easier or harder? What happens? Does the DNA from different fruit look different?

EXTRACT DNA FROM FRUIT!

All the instructions for a living organism are found within its DNA. In this activity, you will extract DNA from fruit. This activity uses similar chemicals and processes that are used to extract DNA in a lab.

- **Add about ⅓ cup of the fruit to the sealable plastic bag.** Remove the air, seal the bag, and then start squishing it up and turn it into paste.

- **Pour ½ cup of water into a clear glass.** Slowly add 2 teaspoons of dish soap and ½ teaspoon of table salt. Gently mix this solution without making bubbles until the salt dissolves. The salt will help the DNA stick together.

- **Add half of this solution to your bag of fruit.** Seal the bag again, removing the air as you do. Gently squish the liquid around. Let this mixture sit for 10 to 20 minutes.

- **Place a coffee filter on top of a clear glass and carefully pour your fruit mixture into the filter.** You can gently squeeze the filter to get more liquid out, just don't break the filter!

- **Tilt the glass and slowly pour the cold alcohol down the side.** You are trying to create a layer of alcohol that floats on the top of the solution. The DNA will come out of the solution as a layer between the water and alcohol. What do you see?

- **Let the solution sit for a few minutes.** Record your observations and make sketches in your science journal. You can collect the DNA using a toothpick or chopstick.

Chapter 4

The People Around You

Who in your life influences your behavior?

Whether you live with biological parents, adoptive parents, grandparents, or family unrelated by blood, the people you see the most are the ones who have the greatest impact on your behavior.

So far, you've learned a lot about the unique physical aspects of what is behind your behavior—your brain, genes, hormones—and some of the environmental influences. But what about the people in your life? How do they contribute to your general psychology?

While you might think of yourself as an individual who knows their own mind and doesn't have to worry about peer pressure, everyone is influenced by the people they hang around with. Whether it's caregivers, friends, classmates, or the celebrities you see on their Instagram stories, other people have a major impact on how you feel and how you behave.

CAREGIVERS

The adult caregivers in your life play a significant role in who you are and how you behave. The family environment provides the basic foundation for how behavior begins to develop and whether it is learned, encouraged, or corrected.

Peer influence during adolescence is greater than ever before. But research has proven that even though the teen years are greatly influenced by peers, adults still serve as the most impactful role models during adolescence for positive and negative behavior.

You are not alone! Check out this video featuring teens talking about the challenges they face in their families. What are some of the challenges you face every day?

 Teens Healthy family

Relationships between teens and caregiving adults can be challenging on both sides. Have you ever felt that the adults in your life just don't understand you? They likely have felt the same way. It can be hard to bridge the emotional gap that hangs between people who see things differently, but caregivers are important in the lives of teens. Adult caregivers serve as role models through actions and words.

Some adults have had poor role models in their own lives. Some struggle with mental health issues or physical illness or deal with addiction. Circumstances such as poverty and geography can also change how a caregiver raises a child. While there is a wide range of parenting styles and capabilities, psychologists recognize three different major categories of parenting—authoritative, authoritarian, and permissive.

Diana Blumberg Baumrind (1927–2018) was a psychologist known for her research in parenting styles. Through extensive observation and interviews, Dr. Baumrind identified three different ways parents tend to raise and guide their children.

Your family is a major part of who you are.

CULTURAL CAREGIVING

Parents raise their children differently based on their culture. American children are generally raised to be independent, competent, and verbally expressive. Japanese parents focus on emotional maturity, self-control, and interdependence. A 2014 report from National Public Radio noted that parents in Argentina let their children stay up all hours of the night, Norwegian parents will leave their sleeping babies in strollers outside a restaurant where they are dining, and French children are taught to eat whatever their parents eat, with no snacks and no substitutions at meal times. How do you feel about some of these cultural differences in parenting?

- Authoritative: The traits of a caregiver raising a child in an authoritative manner include being warm and responsive to a child's needs. Authoritative caregivers have clear rules and high expectations that they convey to the child. They support their children and encourage and value their independence.

Adults who raise kids in this way set boundaries by having open discussions and using reasoning. They are affectionate toward their children and have a good relationship with them.

> Studies indicate that a child with authoritative caregivers will likely have higher grades, a greater sense of self-esteem, and better social skills.

Based on research, children raised in this environment appear happy, content, and more independent. They have better mental health—suffer from less depression and anxiety—and don't get into trouble too often.

- Authoritarian: Adults who raise their children in an authoritarian way have very strict rules, do not respond to their child's needs, and have incredibly high expectations of their children. Caregivers with authoritarian traits also expect children to obey at all times, meaning whatever the caregivers say, goes.

Authoritarian adults tend to say, "Because I said so." They also punish their children to control their behavior. They are usually not very "warm and fuzzy" and don't tend to be nurturing with their children.

Kids who are raised by authoritarian parents are often unhappy, have poorer social skills, and lack self-esteem. Sometimes, they behave more impulsively than others and cause problems both at home and at school.

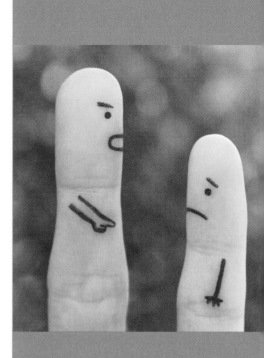

- Permissive: Permissive caregivers, like those who are authoritative, are warm and responsive to children's needs. Permissive caregivers, however, have few rules for children, are lenient with missteps in behavior, and indulge children.

    Based on research, when caregivers are permissive in their style of parenting, their kids sometimes end up being egocentric and impulsive. They may also have poor social skills and problems in their relationships and have a tough time following rules. Self-control can be a foreign concept.

A FOURTH PARENTING STYLE . . . NEGLECTFUL

Stanford psychologists Eleanor Maccoby (1917–2018) and John Martin added another category of parenting style to the three that Dr. Baumrind documented—neglectful parenting, sometimes called uninvolved parenting. Neglectful adults are not loving and do not respond to their children's needs. They are not involved in their children's lives. They are indifferent—they don't seem to care about their children and are more concerned with themselves. They could be this way for a variety of reasons, including their own upbringing, mental health issues, and problems with addiction.

Sometimes, neglectful adults are that way because they are dealing with their own issues, such as alcoholism or other forms of addiction. If this sounds like the adults in your life, learn where to get help and support here.

 Teens Health alcohol

AGGRESSION

Albert Bandura (1925–) is known as one of the most influential psychologists of all time. His social learning theory suggests that new behaviors—such as aggression—can be learned through observation. Dr. Bandura's hypothesis was that children learn aggression through observing and imitating adults or family members who act aggressively. He questioned whether exposure to violent acts would cause children to behave the same way. To test his theory, he invented the Bobo doll experiment in 1961. In this experiment, children were divided into three groups. The control group did not have an adult role model. The second group witnessed an adult being aggressive toward an inflatable Bobo doll, and the third group witnessed a non-aggressive adult with the same doll. The results of the experiment proved that children who observed the aggressive adult model had far more aggressive responses than those who were in the non-aggressive group or the control group.

Watch footage of the famous Bobo doll experiment: What do you think were the results of the study?

 Curious Classroom
Bandura growing up

Whatever the motivation behind neglectful parenting, it can do major harm to children. Many kids who are raised by neglectful parents display impulsive behavior and tend to get into trouble frequently. A greater percentage of them also use drugs and alcohol.

Ideally, children are raised by kind, loving, supportive adults who communicate their expectations and rules with care and consistency.

HELICOPTER PARENTING

Another style of parenting has been getting a lot of attention in the past decade. Dr. Carolyn Daitich, director of the Center for the Treatment of Anxiety Disorders, describes helicopter parenting as "a style of parents who are over-focused on their children." Dr. Daitich states that helicopter parents take too much responsibility for their children's experiences, especially their successes and failures.

According to the results of a study published in 2018 by the American Psychological Association, parents who overcontrol their children can negatively impact the child's ability to manage their own emotions and behavior. What might it feel like to have someone make all your decisions for you?

The study noted that children who have helicopter parents may be less capable of dealing with the challenges of growing up, especially the complexity of the school environment. During the course of eight years, 422 children were studied when they were two years old, again at the age of five, and finally at age 10.

The study revealed that children who were overparented at age two had poorer emotional and behavior regulation at age five. On the flip side, the study showed that the better the five-year-old children were at regulating their emotions, the less likely they were to have emotional problems and the more likely they were to have social skills at the age of 10. The study emphasizes the importance of educating well-intentioned parents about supporting their children's independence in handling their emotional challenges.

ADVERSE CHILDHOOD EXPERIENCES

Adverse childhood experiences (ACEs) include family economic hardship, parental separation or divorce, and living with an abusive caregiver or one who has mental illness. In the 2016 National Survey of Children's Health, results indicated that a large percentage of young people confront challenging experiences in their childhoods.

The study showed that 45 percent of children from birth to the age of 17 in the United States have experienced at least one ACE, and one out of 10 children has experienced three ACEs in their childhood. ACEs can cause stress in children, including feelings of anxiety, fear, and helplessness. ACEs are also linked to increased risk of health issues later in life.

If ACEs occur during a long period of time, toxic levels of stress hormones can impact the physical and emotional growth of a child and even impact the development of the brain.

SITUATIONAL PARENTING

More recent studies describe parenting as being many-sided. A caregiver's actions and reactions may be determined more by a situation than a particular parenting style. Based on this concept, scientists describe parenting based on different child-rearing goals and the various situations parents and children face. Researchers have defined five situationally based parenting styles:

Protection—keeping the child safe from harm

Control—offering societal expectations to a child

Guided learning—teaching specific skills

Group participation—encouraging the child to be part of a social group

Reciprocity—responding to a positive action with a positive reaction

CHILDHOOD TRAUMA

Neuroscientist Ali Jawaid is collecting blood and saliva samples from children in Pakistan, where wars have raged for many years. He is testing both orphaned children and children who still live with their parents. Why? He wants to know if the trauma of separation has caused changes at the cellular level. Many of the orphans have experienced trauma by seeing family members killed in battle. These children experience depression and anxiety similar to posttraumatic stress disorder. Scientists are concerned that the stress these children are experiencing will be passed on genetically to their children and grandchildren.

What can be done for kids who are experiencing tough situations? Policymakers, researchers, pediatric psychologists, and doctors are working together to prevent or address the negative effects of ACEs. As of 2019, 35 states have passed, or have pending, more than 129 bills that mention ACEs.

The American Academy of Pediatrics encourages doctors to regularly screen young children for signs of toxic stress stemming from parental substance abuse, mental health issues, or community violence. Families can be offered support and counseling to help relieve the causes and effects of ACEs.

THE PEOPLE YOU KNOW

Caregivers have crucial input into your behavior, but another group is equally important—peers! Your peers are friends around your own age and even people who are not your friends. These are the people you hang out with at school and on weekends, the kids you might follow on social media, and the ones on the same sports team or in the same drama club.

Have you heard the term "peer pressure"? Peer pressure is feeling as though you need to behave in ways that are similar to the ways your peers behave.

For example, if you are hanging out at a basketball game and a couple of your friends decide to buy some pizza, the rest of the people in the group often decide to do the same thing. When it comes to snacking on pizza, no big deal, right? But what if a few members of the group are vaping? What if they are drinking alcohol?

What if they are engaging in behavior that is risky? Through peer pressure, other members of the group might find themselves making decisions they wouldn't make if they were on their own.

Why do peers have so much power over you? Adolescents are more social than younger children and more social than adults. Teen sociality is all about wanting to belong, to fit into the group. Friends, and what they think of you, are more important at this stage of life than any other.

In Chapter 2, you read how MRI testing showed the effects of peer pressure when teens were asked to imagine what others thought about them. The neurons in the teen brain fired in a way that showed their own sense of self-esteem and self-worth was intricately connected to what other people thought of them. In contrast, adult brains showed adults cared less about the judgment of others.

PSYCH!
\\\\\\\\\\\\\\\\

Teenagers are more vulnerable to peer pressure than any other age group, stemming from their desire for social acceptance.

Vaping is an unhealthy behavior sometimes encouraged through peer pressure.

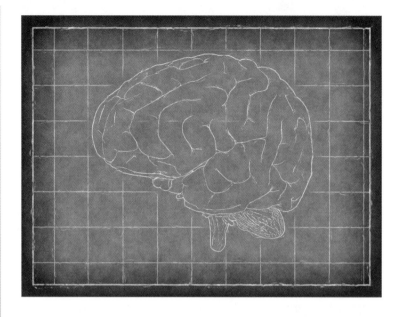

PHYSICAL FOMO

Have you ever felt sick when not included in something? How do you feel when you see a good friend posting a picture from a party you weren't invited to? What might it be like to find tickets to an upcoming concert on your friend's dresser, but she never talked to you about going? What about the time when your group of friends went to get a pizza after the game and didn't include you? It hurts!

Scientific studies led by Dr. Naomi Eisenberger are showing that there is a relationship between social relationships and your physical and emotional well-being.

We all feel better when our connections with our friends are in the right place and physically ill when they aren't. Dr. Eisenberger's studies show social and physical pain share overlapping groups of neurons.

Dr. Eisenberger used a game to study how people respond when being left out. Cyberball is a game originally created by students at Purdue University.

In the Cyberball experiment, someone lies in a brain scanner, believing that they are playing an online game with two other people. In reality, the two other people don't exist, but the person being tested doesn't know that. Each player looks like a spot on the screen, and the three players form a triangle.

The players throw a virtual ball among themselves. The person being studied is choosing who to throw the ball to and assumes the other two are as well. For a while, the ball gets tossed around equally between the three players. And then, the experiment begins as the other two players stop throwing the ball to the person being studied.

When teens realized they were left out of the game, their brains reacted in ways that reflected the hurt from not being included. They felt upset, sad, and angry. They recognized that they were excluded from something, and it didn't feel good to them. It's hard, especially as a teen, to rationalize that it's only a game and not something to feel so bad about.

ADULT ROLE MODELS

Besides caregivers and your peers, others in your life have an influence on your decisions, your behavior, and who you are and will become. During the course of a day, you probably interact with many adults, such as the bus driver, cafeteria worker, or maintenance person at school. But even more, you spend most of your waking hours during the school year with teachers, media specialists, coaches, and club leaders.

Teachers, coaches, and others can have a significant impact on young people's lives, especially if other role models are lacking. Even in families where caregivers are doing a great job, teens can greatly benefit from the attention of other adults they see on a regular basis.

Teachers can influence students not only to work on their academic achievements, but can also encourage them to be better people. A recent study showed that teachers have just as significant an impact on students' academic achievement as they do on their attitudes and behavior.

THE POWER OF SOCIAL MEDIA

The smartphone revolution began at MacWorld 2007 when Steve Jobs (1955–2011) introduced the first iPhone. Now, more than 5 billion people in the world use smartphones. According to the Pew Research Center, more than 96 percent of Americans have a cell phone and 86 percent of millennials use social media.

> Having constant access to social media is impacting our lives and relationships as never before.

A study conducted by the University of Pennsylvania in 2018 connects the use of social media sites such as Facebook, Snapchat, and Instagram to feelings of decreased well-being. Psychologist Melissa G. Hunt concluded through the study that, overall, *less usage* of social media for any age group decreases depression and loneliness.

What's the first thing you do in the morning and the last thing you do at night? If you are like most teens, you check your phone.

Any new text messages? How many people liked your last Instagram post? Is that Snapchat stream still going?

According to marketing experts, teens check their phones up to 150 times a day. That's about nine times an hour! Why? Several recent scientific studies reveal some surprising facts about how much teens (and many adults) rely on cell phones for information and socializing. Let's take a look.

Connection is important, right? And social media is a very powerful tool for connection. But the companionship you might feel through social media isn't the same as sitting and talking with someone face to face. It's different from being part of a group that's involved together in real life.

Many teens who were surveyed also said they are aware of social media's potential to distract them, and that they struggle to monitor their use of social media. In fact, 42 percent of teens admitted social media took them away from hanging out in person with friends. Does this happen to you?

In 2016, a study was conducted at the University of California on the impact of Instagram "likes" on teens' neural and behavioral responses. The researchers wanted to determine how peer influence occurs on social media.

Using functional MRI to simulate Instagram, they measured adolescents' behavioral and neural responses to likes, which are a form of social endorsement and a potential source of peer influence. The results of the study reflect that participants showed greater neural activity when viewing photos with more likes. Plus, adolescents were more likely to like a photo if it already had many likes—even if the photo showed risky behaviors.

SOCIAL MEDIA SURVEY

In November 2018, the Pew Research Center published a report called "Teens' Social Media Habits and Experiences." Teens shared that, although social media helps build stronger friendships and diversifies their world, they were also concerned about exposure to drama and social pressure. Specifically, 45 percent felt overwhelmed by all the drama on social media, 43 percent felt pressure to post only things that made them look good, and 37 percent felt pressure to post content that gets a lot of likes and comments from their followers and friends.

Teens included in the study also shared that they often unfriend or unfollow someone because of cyberbullying, even if they weren't the target.

CYBERBULLYING

What do you consider to be cyberbullying? Mental health experts define it as sending or posting negative, mean, or false content about someone else on the internet with the intent to harm them. Cyberbullying can also include posting private information about someone, intending to shame them. Sometimes, cyberbullying can cross over the line into criminal acts such as harassment, committing hate crimes, or sexting. Have you ever been cyberbullied? Have you been the one to inflict the pain on someone else? Studies show about one in five teens is a victim of this hurtful behavior. Cyberbullying is associated with depression, anxiety, and an elevated risk of suicidal thoughts and even suicide. Be sure to get help from an adult if you or people you know are being cyberbullied.

Go to this website for help with preventing or avoiding cyberbullying.

 cyberbully help

Have you ever found yourself liking a photo just because many others had liked it?

Teens aren't the only ones using social media and smartphones. Studies show that 90 percent of millennials (ages 23–38), 90 percent of Gen Xers (ages 39–54), 68 percent of baby boomers (ages 55–73), and 40 percent of what is known as the silent generation (ages 74–91) use smartphones. While the percentage of millennials using social media has remain unchanged since 2012, all other age groups have used social media at least 10 percent more than previously recorded, according to a report from the Pew Research Center.

A cell phone and all of its applications and uses has many benefits. Socialization and information provided at our fingertips can be a means to building our confidence. But cell phones should also come with a warning label. Too much exposure can lend itself to higher anxiety, depression, and a lack of sleep.

The key is to watch the amount of time spent online and with social media. Self-monitoring apps can help you focus your time and encourage you to take breaks from your devices.

Some schools ban cell phones to help students with their studies and keep on task. For example, according to *Education Week*, more than 30 school districts across the country have banned the usage of cell phones during school hours. Many other districts have restrictions on the use of smartphones during school hours. Banning cell phones isn't as easy as it sounds. Enforcing the ban can be difficult, and school districts are hesitant to take responsibility for a student's confiscated phone.

Some schools use apps to teach students healthy, responsible smartphone habits as opposed to banning phones entirely.

One important objection to cell phone bans is safety. In the case of an emergency, such as a school lockdown or dangerous weather, students would not be able to communicate with their caregivers. Common Sense Media, an organization that focuses on children, technology, and media, encourages schools to "Have a plan, not a ban" when it comes to student smartphone usage during the school day.

What is your school district's policy on phone usage? Do you agree with these policies? What would you do differently?

Your peers—both online and in real life—have a huge influence on what you do. In the next chapter, we'll take a deeper dive into how people behave in groups vs. how they behave alone.

KEY QUESTIONS

- **What type of parenting style do you think your caregivers use? How has their parenting style affected you?**

- **Do you have a teacher who is making a positive impact in your life?**

STORYBOARD YOUR STORY!

Knowing who you are and what is important to you helps when you are faced with options that might not seem to be the best choice for you. In this activity, you will explore the significance of you!

- **Fold a piece of paper into eight sections.**

- **Draw out your life journey.** Make it simple, using stick figures and no words.

- **Include elements such as family, likes/dislikes, extracurricular activities, and any major life events.** Make sure to highlight all the special aspects of you!

- **Throughout the exercise, make sure to include significant events in your life.** What challenges have you been through? What have you succeeded at? What are you really good at? What have you accomplished? Was there ever a situation that was difficult to overcome, but you did? What about a situation that maybe you could have handled better? How have these experiences shaped you as a person?

- **Share the storyboard with a friend.**

To investigate more, discuss what shapes self-identity. How does being aware of your self-identity influence your life choices, particularly in friendships? How have your choices and perspectives changed from when you were younger?

Chapter 5

Flocking Together: Behavior in Groups

Do you behave differently in groups from when you are alone?

Studies have shown that people's behavior does change depending on whether they are alone or surrounded by other people. A variety of factors contributes to this!

Look around your table in the school cafeteria, at a party, or wherever your peer group gathers. Are you wearing clothes similar to your friends'? Do you all style your hair the same way? Think about the memes you share, the games you play, and the movies you watch. Chances are good that the people around the table have much the same tastes in the media they consume.

When you think about individual behaviors within a group, it gets even more interesting.

Do you know of groups of friends who decide to ditch class to get fast food? Have you ever been in that situation? Did you jump on board and skip out without giving it much thought? You weren't alone—literally! Social psychology is the study of how we think about, influence, and relate to one another. Let's explore this more.

ASCH CONFORMITY EXPERIMENTS

Imagine that you are invited by a friend to be part of a psychology experiment after school one day. You show up at the designated classroom with your friend. Six other students you've never met are waiting, too. What you don't know is that the rest of the students are in on a secret. They are there to try to get you to agree to their answers on a test, even though they are clearly wrong. That's the psychology experiment.

An adult enters the room with two pieces of poster board in her hands. One poster board has a single, vertical line. The other poster board has three vertical lines, of different lengths. She asks each of you to say which line in the set of three matches the length of the single line on the first poster board.

 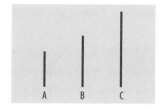

The answer is line B, yet, one by one, each of the other students answers C. Huh? While you are sitting there, your mind starts to play tricks on you. Is it really C? How can they all be so wrong? What answer do you give?

Dr. Solomon Asch (1907–1996), a pioneer in the field of social psychology, conducted this same experiment back in the 1950s. His studies revealed that, on average, about one-third of the test subjects answered the same as the rest of the group, even knowing the answer was wrong.

"Groupthink" is a term that social psychologist Irving L. Janis (1918–1980) came up with. Groupthink is a psychological phenomenon that can occur when people try for consensus within a group. Often people will set aside their own thoughts and personal beliefs and adopt those of the group, which can lead to incorrect conclusions.

Of the 12 trials he conducted, 75 percent of the participants conformed at least once, while 25 percent never conformed. When the participants were interviewed after the experiment, most said that they went along with the group out of fear of being ridiculed. Others said they went along with the group because they decided the group's answers were correct and that they were wrong.

Why did this happen? Have you ever felt the need to conform while in a group? Like most of our behavior, group behavior has its roots in our brains.

NEUROSCIENCE OF GROUP BEHAVIOR

Scientists have studied the development of the brain from childhood through adulthood to discover how people react to certain situations, including within a group setting. Both psychologists and neuroscientists have tried to gain insight into our behavioral impulses and our control over them. These impulses are defined as "approach" and "avoidance." What makes us go toward something (approach) or stay away from something (avoid)?

Researchers have determined that approach/avoidance behavior is made up of automatically triggered, unconscious processes and more consciously controlled reactions. Again, this comes down to the prefrontal cortex, which oversees approach/avoid behavior. A fully developed adult brain can decide whether to approach or avoid based on reasoned choices. In a teen, that function isn't fully developed.

When group dynamics enter the picture, a teenager may have awareness of risky behaviors, but group influence may override that awareness.

POWER OF GROUPS

As we saw in the Asch experiments, people of all ages can be led to conform in groups, even in the face of inaccurate information. Why is this? Conformity within a group feels safe. It feels as though we are liked. It might seem better to be part of a group that's wrong than stand alone knowing you're right.

One common refrain from people who are questioning the behavior of teens is, "If everyone jumped off a cliff, would you jump, too?"

"Groupthink" is a term used for groups that sometimes make an irrational or misguided decision based on that urge to conform. The decision may be simply a result of the members preferring harmony over rational thinking. Group members may decide to not express differences in opinions or doubts because they don't want to stand out or risk unacceptance.

GROUP DYNAMICS IN MEDICINE

Health care providers can take advantage of working as a group to better serve their patients. Studies conducted in 2015 showed that when a majority of independent dermatologists agreed on skin and breast cancer diagnoses, they were correct more often than they were as individuals. What kind of implications might this have for the future of medical care? What about other fields? Do you think a house design voted on by a majority of architects would be better than one designed by an individual? What space does this leave for individual genius?

MOB MENTALITY

Hundreds of people rise up in protest against political leaders. Thousands of concert fans sing along to their favorite artist, lit cell phones in hand, swaying to the music. Would these individuals act the same way without the influence of the crowd? Not necessarily. Humans imitate the behavior of other people. We act out in ways that we might not on our own. Psychologists define this type of behavior as mob mentality, or herd mentality. Have you ever been caught up in talking badly about someone and it seemed natural because everyone else in the group was doing so? Mob mentality happens when people adopt behaviors, follow trends, and make choices based on the influence of others. It demonstrates how people's points of view can be swallowed up by those who surround us. Mob mentality can work in positive ways, to make change, to make a difference—or it can work in negative ways. Watch what happens when 60,000 people wait together for a Green Day concert to start.

🔍 Green Day crowd Queen

Have you ever felt uncomfortable stating your opinion in a group? What was it like? Were you able to stand apart?

Group dynamics has an upside, though. It usually makes sense to pool information, right? When you're working in a group and all the members care about doing well and contribute their knowledge and talents, you can do great things!

Experiments have shown that in both small groups and larger groups, combining the information given by the individual participants resulted in information that was closer to the truth. This is because it was based on many inputs.

EVERYONE NEEDS SUPPORT

Peers and friend groups are vital sources of feedback for everyone. Whether you have one or two friends or a much larger network, interactions with other people is how we learn about ourselves.

Friends introduce each other to new activities, such as sports or volunteering, that expand horizons and offer new challenges. We come to a better understanding of ourselves through new activities, and those new hobbies could even turn into careers.

Another benefit of groups is emotional support. According to Dr. Robert M. Sapolsky (1957–), professor of biology and neurology at Stanford University, teens excel at empathy, the ability to feel someone else's pain and to try to make everything right—more so than any other age group.

Why? Because of their vast inventory of emotions and openness to new situations and people.

Friends and peers can lend emotional support to you as strongly as you do to them. Because their capacity to feel is as strong as yours, friends can be a big factor in your emotional support.

EQUAL WORK?

Group dynamics and the influence peers can have on behavior can have downsides, too. Conformity is yielding to group pressure, which humans at any age do. When participating in groups, sometimes individuals don't contribute as much as they would if doing the work independently. And sometimes, humans make wrong choices just because everyone else is doing so.

Have you ever been involved in a group project and someone simply wasn't pulling their weight? On the flip side, have you ever felt lazy and not contributed as much as you should? Social loafing is a term used to describe the tendency of individuals to put in less effort when a large group is involved. When all members contribute their efforts toward a common goal, each member contributes less than they would if they were responsible for the entire project.

Scientists have determined several reasons for this. If the group participants aren't motivated by the task, the chance of social loafing is greater. Have you ever worked on a group project at school and weren't that interested in the topic? Did you still do your fair share of the work?

Often, participants in a larger group feel less responsibility and may decide that their individual contributions don't make a difference to the results. Individuals in smaller groups, however, are likely to participate more. And, finally, if members of a group expect others to slack off, they likely will.

Check out this Brain Games video on conformity. Was that standing ovation deserved?

 Brain Game conformity

INDEPENDENCE

Have you ever heard the phrase, "cutting the apron strings?" This refers to a caregiver loosening their ties on older children and allowing more freedom away from home and the family. Teens tend to naturally have more time away from adults as a result of school, afterschool activities, and work—this is a normal thing. It's part of the process of becoming a fully independent adult.

When individual responsibility is spread out through a group, the bystander effect might come into play. For decades, scientists believed that the bystander effect happened when the presence of other people discouraged someone from helping out in an emergency situation. Researchers conducted studies that seemed to show the larger the group of bystanders, the less likely it was any one person would step up.

Observations of real-life emergencies, though, have shown that people in crowds do help.

UNDER PRESSURE

The teen years are a time when people are separating more from family relationships and spending more time with friends and peers. Remember, studies have shown that teens care more about what others think of them than any other age group. What does this mean for behavior?

The stoplight task, developed in 1979, was a simple, simulated driving task in which teens controlled the movement of a vehicle along a straight track from the driver's point of view. Each round had 20 intersections, which took under 6 minutes to travel through. As the vehicle approached each intersection, the traffic signal turned yellow and the teen had to decide by pressing a button whether to go through the intersection and risk a possible crash or to brake and wait for the light to return to green.

Importantly, both the timing of the traffic signals and the potential of a crash at the intersections varied, so the participant couldn't predict them.

Risk-taking—for example, not braking for the yellow light—was encouraged by the monetary incentives participants were given for completing the course as quickly as possible. Successfully traveling through an intersection without braking saved time, whereas braking and waiting for the signal to turn green again added time. If the participant did not brake and a crash occurred, even more time was piled on.

In 2011, the teens being tested completed four rounds—two alone and two when they knew their friends were watching from another room. The results? Adolescents took a significantly greater number of risks when they knew they were being observed by peers than when alone. Scientists had predicted this outcome and they were right about the neuroscience behind it as well. The test subjects were measured through fMRI, which showed activity in areas of the brain involved in reward processing when peers were present.

Texting while driving is a risk that has minimal short-term reward and potential long-term consequences.

In the 1960s, social psychologists Bibb Latané (1937–) and John Darley (1938–2018) researched the concept of the bystander effect following the infamous murder of Kitty Genovese (1935–1964) in New York City. As 28-year-old Genovese was stabbed to death outside her apartment, neighbors failed to step in to assist or call the police. The scientists wondered why this could be and conducted a series of experiments. The conclusion was that people were less likely to help when they perceived that more individuals were witness to a situation. But as we've seen, scientific theories change with time, experimentation, and observation. Now, it's generally accepted that the bystander effect isn't real. What other scientific theories have changed as a result of deeper inquiry?

PSYCH!

\\\\\\\\\\\\\\\\\\\\\\\\\

Due to the effect other passengers have on young drivers, many states have laws regarding how many passengers can be in the car with newly licensed drivers. Your state laws may not allow you to have any passengers under the age of 20 unless you have someone over the age of 25 accompanying you.

Check out this video to learn more about standing up to manipulation from peers!

 beh sci guys manipulation

The experiment featured the joint contribution of the two brain systems that affect decision-making: the incentive processing system, which involves primarily the ventral striatum, and the cognitive control system, including the lateral prefrontal cortex (LPFC). The ventral striatum sways the decisions people make by weighing potential rewards and punishments. The LPFC supports decision-making by keeping impulses in balance and by providing the mental equipment necessary for considering other choices.

PEER PRESSURE

What does all of this data mean when it comes to making decisions about drugs and alcohol and other risky behavior? According to the 2017 National Survey on Drug Use and Health Study, about 7.4 million Americans between the ages of 12 and 20 report drinking alcohol. That's about 20 percent of this age group, all of whom are under legal drinking age. The upside is that 80 percent of teens in this age group surveyed are not using alcohol.

Another area of potential risky behavior is sex. Scientists recently conducted a study on whether teens were becoming sexually active based on their perceptions of their friends doing the same. At the outset of the study, the scientists noted that not all teens were susceptible to peer influence. So, they set out to figure out who might be more influenced by their peers.

The study involved 300 seventh- and eighth-grade students, with an average age of 12.6. Before the experiment, each adolescent was assessed on demographics, attitudes toward sex, and hypothetical situations measuring the likelihood of the student taking part in risky sexual behavior.

Then, the students took part in what they believed to be an internet chat room where their peers were talking about the same hypothetical situations that were reviewed in the pre-experiment assessment. This meant that the students were first asked about their involvement with sex privately, then asked again while other students were involved in the discussion. Would you answer the questions the same way in both scenarios? Do you think the students involved in the study did?

> In turned out that 78 percent of those involved in the experiment provided more risky answers in the chat room than in the pretest. These kids were susceptible to peer pressure.

The study suggests that teens may talk about having sex, but in reality, most aren't yet sexually active. According to the Guttmacher Institute, age 18 is the average of a first sexual experience in the United States.

Your peers are important in many aspects of your mental health. In the next chapter, we'll take a look at how stress can affect everything in your life, including your relationships.

KEY QUESTIONS

- Have you ever felt manipulated into making a decision you didn't feel comfortable with?
- When faced with a decision in a group, did you go along with the crowd or stand up for your beliefs?
- Were you ever in a situation where you did cave to peer pressure and you wish you hadn't?

We've seen how people think differently within a group, even when they know they are right and the others are wrong. Do you have a choice? Is the group simply too powerful? You always have a choice, as uncomfortable as it might be. And often, when one person breaks the pattern of groupthink, more people follow suit and change their opinions to reflect their true beliefs.

Check out a conformity experiment in action in this video. If you were in the room, how do you think you would respond?

VitalSmarts Video peer pressure

TEXT TO WORLD

How might the benefits and perils of groupthink be applied to your country's politics?

CONFORMING EXPERIMENT

The Asch Conformity Tests proved that, on average, a third of a group would answer a question incorrectly, based on the influence of others, even when they knew otherwise. To explore this behavior through conformity tests, try the following experiments.

- **Recruit a few friends to stand in a shopping mall.** They should just stare at the ceiling.

- **Make a grid in a notebook.** Record how many people stop and stare with the group within 15 minutes. How many people pass by without participating in the behavior? Record these results and compare your study to the Asch Conformity Test. Did a third of the people walking past in the mall look up to the ceiling as well?

- **Recruit your math teacher and a few friends to help out in class.** Have the teacher ask a multiplication question, such as what is 9 x 4? Have her ask the friends who are in on the experiment to answer the question incorrectly. Perhaps they all answer the question with the incorrect number of 32. Record how many students offer that same response instead of the correct answer of 36. Were the results similar to your ceiling test?

> To investigate more, interview your test subjects after the experiments if possible. Do they know why they conformed in the group setting? If any of them did not conform, can they address their experiences? What would they do differently the next time they are faced with a similar situation?

Chapter 6 ▶
When Bad Stuff Happens

What makes you
stressed in your life?

We all experience
stress and hardship in
life—it's unavoidable!
How we deal with
the stress can
help determine
our overall health
and development.
And when the
stress gets really
bad, it's important
to ask for help.

We all experience stress. You might feel stressed because of an upcoming test, a fight with a friend, or your family is moving. Some people have stress in their lives because of abuse, addiction, or other hardships. And just as there are different levels of stress, there are many different individual responses to stress. One person might deal with stress far differently from another person.

But what exactly is stress? Stress in humans happens when mental, emotional, and physical demands are beyond our ability to handle. Do you feel different when you are having an argument or other drama with a friend? What about when an adult is mad at you—does that stress you out?

Being stressed out might give you a stomachache or a headache or produce extra sweat on your body. It might mean you want to curl up and sleep or make you lash out at other people.

It's uncomfortable.

Stress might seem like a mental issue, but the body is affected as well. Homeostasis describes the state of our bodies when all the body's systems are in balance. Stressors, or anything and anyone who causes us to experience stress, affects our homeostatic balance.

The impact of stress depends on how significant, frequent, and prolonged the stress is. While we can adapt to moderate levels of stress, too much stress can have negative consequences on our emotional, mental, and physical well-being. Being stressed about a math test is much different from being stressed about failing math for the year. And being stressed about the death of someone close to you is a whole other level of stress.

Scientific studies have shown that chronic stress—stress that occurs for a long time or keeps recurring—can even change the gray and white matter of the brain, affecting the neural connections.

Our brains can actually become rewired based on continual and significant stress.

Check out this cool video on the importance and process of homeostasis.

 homeostasis fuse school

OVERWHELMING

Suicide is the third-leading cause of death in young people ages 15 to 24. Teens and young adults experience a lot of stress. Major changes are happening in their bodies, their minds, relationships, and families. Normal developmental changes can be overwhelming when combined with other serious changes, such as divorce, a move, a death, changes in friendships, and cyberbullying. Warning signs for suicidal behavior include loss of interest in regular activities, changes in sleeping and eating habits, and feelings of wanting to die. If you or someone you know is feeling this way, get help. Talk to the school counselor, the school resource officer, or a teacher. You can also call 911. It could mean the difference between life and death.

Check out this video on stress and chronic stress.

stress
bergquist

PSYCH!

〰〰〰〰〰〰〰〰〰〰〰

Have you heard of Vital Scout? It is a personal monitor and app that 24/7 measures your stress and recovery rate from stress. A simple patch is attached to your body and records your heart rate and variances based on your activities. Scientists at Stanford University are using the patch to study the connection between stress and depression in teens.

We all have stress in our lives. How much is too much? Let's explore.

THE DIFFERENT LEVELS OF STRESS

The American Psychological Association has defined three levels of stress, based on the situation, the duration, and the impact on our bodies. These levels of stress are acute stress, episodic acute stress, and chronic stress.

Acute stress is the type of stress we all experience every day, often several times a day. This is the least damaging to our bodies. It is the type of stress experienced when we perceive an immediate threat. The threat may be real or imagined, but it's the recognition of the danger that triggers the stress response.

Can stress be good? Sure! Most people love stress that is exciting, that gives us an adrenaline rush, and that reminds us it's exciting to be alive. It's the feeling you get at a baseball game when a foul ball comes flying toward you, only to be stopped by the safety net. Phew!

Acute stress is mild. It's part of our everyday life. Acute stressors include the alarm clock going off while you are in deep sleep, a new homework assignment due tomorrow, or a near accident while driving. Sometimes, acute stress can be more serious, too, such as getting into an argument with a friend, being surprised by a pop quiz, or getting detention at school. Acute stress is the everyday kind of experience, such as forgetting a homework assignment or leaving your basketball shoes at home.

This level of stress is something most people can manage fairly easily. And it isn't always a negative thing for our bodies. Do you like roller coasters? That's acute stress you're feeling!

Acute stress doesn't have any ongoing, negative affects to the body. In fact, episodes of acute stress help us to learn to work through future stressful situations.

You might notice some physical changes to your body. How do you feel when a test is handed out at school? Most people respond with some extra sweating and an increased heart rate. This is your body's natural response to stress—it's known as the fight-or-flight response, which we'll explore in a bit. It's a natural process that can actually keep you safe in a possibly dangerous situation.

> When acute stress happens too often,
> it becomes episodic acute stress.

A person experiencing episodic acute stress feels continually overwhelmed and as though life is filled with mini crises. A person feeling this form of stress may have too many activities, too many deadlines, and just too many things going on in their lives at the same time.

This kind of stress is more intense. For instance, a teen might be taking college-prep courses while participating in a sport and jazz band and volunteering at the food pantry every week. That's a lot of stress. Perhaps an adult has a work situation where they are assigned too many work projects at the same time.

Someone experiencing episodic acute stress always feels pressured and rushed.

Feeling stressed about school? You're not alone. Check out this article on teens, stress, and school.

 KidsHealth school stress

Check out this video featuring teens talking about stress.

 KidsHealth teen stress

As time goes by, this continual form of acute stress can take its toll on relationships, health, school, and work.

The third form of stress, chronic stress, is a constant, unending stress. Chronic stress can result from financial issues, divorce, death of a loved one, or unhealthy relationships. Chronic stress can do the most physical harm to our bodies.

This is the worst type of stress. Poverty, divorce, a bad job, a rough time in school, and unhealthy relationships are all stressors that can lead to a chronic state. Loneliness or lack of relationships can also contribute to chronic stress.

Deeper levels of stress can also result from having witnessed or been victim of terrible circumstances. Abuse, addiction, abandonment, and many other damaging situations cause intense stress. The longer these last, the harder it can be to recover and feel healthy and well again.

In fMRI studies conducted at the Stress and Development Lab at Harvard University, researchers looked at the brains of children who had been exposed to or were victims of abuse, domestic violence, or violence in their communities. They compared them to the brains of children who hadn't been exposed to this kind of stress. When viewing negative emotional stimuli, the brain response of children who had experienced childhood adversity was much higher in the amygdala—the emotional response center—than in those children who hadn't experienced childhood adversity.

WHAT'S UP IN THE BODY?

Dr. Walter Cannon (1871–1945) was a physiologist, a doctor who studies the functions and activities of living matter, such as cells and organs. While studying swallowing and digestion in rats in the laboratory, he discovered that when rats were frightened or startled, a process called peristalsis suddenly stopped. Peristalsis is the process that helps move food forward through the body during digestion. The rats were demonstrating a natural response to a dangerous or frightening situation, which Dr. Cannon called the fight-or-flight response.

STRESSORS IN AMERICA

Many Americans are experiencing chronic stress. Mass shootings are one example of an environmental stress factor that can lead to chronic stress. As *The Washington Post* reported, 220,000 children from 225 schools have witnessed a school shooting since the Columbine High School incident in 1999. In the 2018 American Psychological Association report, younger adults ages 15 to 21 reported that their mental health was just fair, or even poor. The survey also found that this age group was more likely to report that current issues were causing them more stress than adults were experiencing. Headlines that carry news of mass shootings brought stress to more than 70 percent of this age group. Is this something you feel stress about? If so, what kinds of things do you do to deal with the stress? You'll learn more about dealing with stress in the next chapter.

PSYCH!

The hypothalamic pituitary adrenal (HPA) axis is our central response system to stress.

Check out this informational video on the symptoms and strategies to manage PTSD.

 YouTube strategies kids PTSD

 PS

Here's a great article on the stress response!

fontiers have no fear

PS

And guess what? Human bodies do the same thing. Dr. Cannon was the first scientist to investigate our body's response to emotion.

When you feel stressed, you are likely to start breathing heavily and you might feel your heart beating hard in your chest. If you're facing physical confrontation, you might run away from the situation or put your arms up, fists raised, ready to fight. You might also simply freeze up, not certain what to do. Any guesses as to where all the responses come from?

Your brain is in control of your stress response! Remember the amygdala and the prefrontal cortex? Well, they fire up big time when you experience a stressful situation. The amygdala recognizes the stress and the prefrontal cortex helps determine how you react to an event.

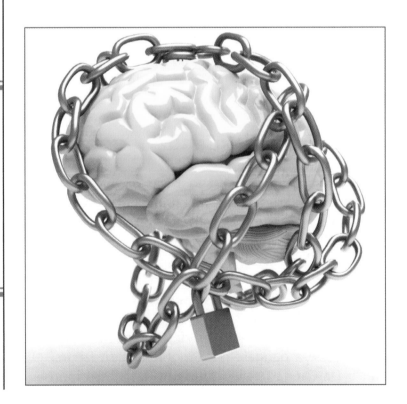

From there, the hypothalamus in the brain and the pituitary and adrenal glands jump on the bandwagon. Together, these are called the HPA axis.

The hypothalamus lets the pituitary gland know that you are experiencing stress. In turn, the hormones created by the pituitary gland let the adrenal glands know to release cortisol. Cortisol is known as the stress hormone. Cortisol has a big job to do—it helps you figure out how dangerous a situation is and then sends energy to your muscles and increases your heart rate and breathing.

All these responses can help you if you need to make a quick exit or if you have to defend yourself. But sometimes, your body might just freeze up.

Along with increased heart rate and faster breathing, humans face these other physical symptoms when facing a stressful situation.

- Pale or flushed skin. Your blood flow is reduced from your body's surface and focused toward the muscles. Even more fascinating is that your blood's clotting ability is increased, in case of bodily injury. It's like your own coat of armor!

- Dilated pupils. You gain a super-power as your body becomes hyperaware of your surroundings and your pupils dilate, which results in better vision.

- Trembling. Have you ever felt your body shake in a frightening situation? That's your muscles' reaction to the stress, ultimately getting ready to react.

- Increased insulin. This hormone is secreted at higher levels to help boost your energy.

POSTTRAUMATIC STRESS DISORDER

According to the American Psychiatric Association, posttraumatic stress disorder (PTSD) is a psychiatric disorder that can occur in people who have experienced or witnessed a traumatic event, such as a natural disaster, a serious accident, a terrorist act, war or combat, rape, or other violent personal assault. Scientists have learned that when a child is exposed to such trauma, such exposure may lead to mental health issues. Those who experience the highest levels of trauma are four times more likely to develop a mental disorder than children who do not have those experiences.

Check out this video on ways to work through mental health issues, as told by teens.

 Amer Acad child mental health

ANHEDONIA

The effects of stress are bound to have an impact on behavior, given that the brain circuits affected by stress control different aspects of behavior. In adolescents, scientists have focused on a specific state known as anhedonia. This is the inability to experience feelings of pleasure in response to things you used to find fun and rewarding. Anhedonia is associated with several disorders, including depression and substance abuse disorder. In other words, as a result of the damage caused by chronic stress, we may feel clinically depressed, or we may seek and abuse substances to bring pleasure, because we don't experience pleasure naturally.

After the situation is no longer stressful, your body returns to normal, the state known as homeostasis.

For years, scientists believed that the physical responses when facing a situation were either fight or flight. Then a third typical response was recognized, known as tonic immobility—or more simply, "freezing." Sometimes, when a situation is incredibly threatening, our reaction is to become numb, seemingly unable to move.

Has your dog ever stumbled upon a small herd of deer in the woods? At first, all of them freeze. Then, they bolt. Maybe you can relate to having been caught doing something you weren't supposed to be doing, such as borrowing money from your dad's wallet. When caught in the action, you likely froze.

These are all physical reactions to stress or threatening situations. And when the stress is extreme, your body responds with another set of bodily responses. We'll learn more about these in the following section.

DEPRESSION

There are various levels of depression. Minor depression symptoms include irritability, negative thoughts, extreme tiredness, a sense of hopelessness, difficulty focusing, feeling unmotivated, and just wanting to be left alone. Often, symptoms of minor depression can be lessened or alleviated with proper care, including talking to caregivers, friends, or a counselor. When symptoms of depression increase and get worse to include constant worrying or nonstop frustration, a person might be experiencing moderate depression.

In this case, professional counseling might be the best solution. A psychologist or psychiatrist can find a therapy that works for an individual.

Major depression, also known as clinical depression, is sometimes linked to chronic stress. Depression is a mood disorder that involves our bodies, moods, and thoughts. Our eating, sleeping, and thinking patterns can be affected by depression.

> Being clinically depressed doesn't mean that we can just "snap out of" our feelings of sadness.

It is not a sign of personal weakness nor is it something that just goes away. Treatment is often necessary and many times crucial to recovery.

Here are a few facts about depression from the National Institute of Mental Health.

- Research indicates that depression is occurring earlier in life today than in past decades.

- When depression occurs in childhood, the depression often persists, recurs, and continues into adulthood. Depression in youth may also predict more severe mental illness in adulthood.

- Adolescents whose parents experience depression are more likely to become depressed than adolescents whose parents do not experience depression.

Traumatic events and experiences can impact you so significantly that you become depressed. But several other factors may also increase your risk for depression. Genetics can play a factor. Do you have any family members who are challenged with a depressive illness? If so, you may be more inclined to be clinically depressed.

SMARTPHONES AND DEPRESSION

Is your cell phone causing you to be depressed? Scientists and parents alike are looking into the effects your cell phone might have on your ability to think, remember, pay attention, be mindful of your surroundings, and regulate your emotions. A recent study of more than half a million young people from eighth to twelfth grades found that the number of kids experiencing high levels of depressive symptoms increased by 33 percent between 2010 and 2015. Smartphones were introduced in 2007, and by 2015, 92 percent of teens and young adults owned one. Do you see the correlation? One of the biggest differences in the lives of today's teenagers, compared to earlier generations, is that they spend less time connecting in person and more time connecting online. This might contribute to increased rates of depression.

It could also mean that more kids are getting the diagnoses they need now than in earlier times. Correlation does not always mean causation.

Plus, medical conditions such as thyroid disorders, anemia, diabetes, and chronic disease or pain can contribute to depression. If you have a family history of any significant medical conditions, be sure to talk to your doctor. Depression can also result from a sense of low self-esteem or feeling alone or left out.

If you feel as though you may be depressed, get help. Many resources are available to you, from a school counselor to therapists who specialize in working with children.

STRESS AND SUBSTANCE ABUSE

While there are plenty of healthy ways to deal with stress, there are also plenty of unhealthy ways. One of those is substance abuse. Scientists have learned that stress is a key risk factor in the use of drugs, sometimes resulting in relapsing, addiction, and ultimately, treatment failure.

According to the 2016 National Survey on Drug Use and Health, 3.1 million adolescents had a major depressive episode in 2016. Of those, about 330,000 were dealing with a substance abuse disorder as well. Teens who use illegal substances before the age of 14 are at the greatest risk of substance dependence, with a 34 percent chance of battling a lifetime of substance use and abuse.

According to the Centers for Disease Control and Prevention, in 2016, an estimated 18 percent of people aged 12 years and older in the United States reported using illicit drugs or misusing prescription drugs in the previous year. Why do people turn to drugs? Their psychological, environmental, and genetic predisposition, along with stress, can be a major part of the reason.

Alcohol and drugs may serve as a form of relief for people who are under chronic stress. These substances can be numbing. They offer a kind of escape. But these destructive habits actually make the damage that stress causes on someone's physical and mental well-being worse. Substance abuse can include serious negative consequences—car accidents, delinquency from school or work, strained personal relationships. Abusing drugs or alcohol only perpetuates the problems brought on by stress.

Keep reading to discover healthier ways to work through the tough stuff that happens in life.

KEY QUESTIONS

- **What type of stress do you have in your life?**
- **What are some of the things you do to work through stress that you experience?**
- **What are some ways you can help other people who are going through a hard time?**

VOCAB LAB

Write down what you think each word means. What root words can you find to help you? What does the context of the word tell you?

acute stress, chronic stress, episodic acute stress, depression, and **posttraumatic stress disorder (PTSD).**

Compare your definitions with those of your friends or classmates. Did you all come up with the same meanings? Turn to the text and glossary if you need help.

TEXT TO WORLD

What does an increase in a stressed population mean for a city's social services? What is the connection between an individual's mental health and a city's financial health?

PSYCH!

The term FOMO, or fear of missing out, was added to the Oxford English Dictionary in 2013. The feeling of being left out isn't new, but due to the increased use of social media, teens are experiencing this at significantly higher levels than ever before.

To investigate more, consider what might happen if you went an entire day without your phone. How do you think you would feel? What do you think you would do instead of checking your phone? Try it and see!

STRESS AND THE SMARTPHONE

Can you imagine being without your phone for an hour during the day? How about two? What about a whole day? How would you feel? Do you think you would feel more stress or less? Let's investigate!

- **You'll need 10 friends to volunteer to give up their phones during the lunch hour at school.** Make sure your friends let their caregivers know they won't be accessible during the experiment.

- **Turn all the cell phones off.** Have someone responsible collect all the phones and keep them safe.

- **Have each participant record how many times they think about checking their phone.**

- **Create a graph noting how many times each participant wanted to check their phone.**

  - What was the average number of times participants thought about checking their phones?

  - How did it make them feel when they weren't able to? Anxious or relieved? Ask them to rate their level of anxiety on a scale of one to ten. Ask them to rate their feeling of freedom on the same scale.

- **Now, have the volunteers surrender their phones for another hour.**

  - What was the average number of times participants thought about checking their phones during the second hour? Was this more or less than the first hour?

  - Did participants report feeling more or less anxious or happy during the second hour?

Chapter 7 ▶
Healthy Body, Healthy Mind

How can people take care of themselves so they feel better mentally, physically, and emotionally?

Scientists are learning more every day about direct correlations between better mental health and eating right, exercising, getting enough sleep, and seeking professional help when necessary. Mindful exercises such as yoga and meditation are proving to help as well.

What can you do to fuel your brain and body? What steps can you take to reduce the stress in your life? How might you present the very best versions of yourself to the world and live your best, most fulfilling life? While it might seem that nutrition, exercise, and sleep are all topics that relate only to physical health, scientists continue to discover that physical health is directly connected to mental and emotional health.

The choices you make in terms of food, fitness, and sleep have a major impact on how you feel beyond headaches or stomachaches. Let's start with food. How does what you eat contribute to how you feel?

YOU ARE WHAT YOU EAT

Nutritional psychology is a relatively new field. Experts study the relationship between what we eat and how we behave and have discovered that eating healthy foods is not only good for our physical health, but also our mental well-being.

Within the last decade, scientists have proved a direct correlation in adults between overall diet quality and depression and anxiety. These studies suggest that a healthy diet consisting of lots of fruits, vegetables, fish, and whole grains is associated with a reduced chance of depression.

Researchers are also investigating connections between healthy diets and the reduced likelihood of mental health issues in children and adolescents.

On the flip side, scientists have confirmed that unhealthy dietary habits are associated with mental health problems. These relationships between food and mood are usually shown to be independent of other health-related behaviors, such as physical activity and smoking, and are also independent of environmental health factors, such as socioeconomic status, conflicts within the family, and poor family functioning. In other words, a healthy diet might overcome other mental health factors that we don't have control over.

A healthy diet is especially important for our brains. Our brains are always working, even when we are sleeping. Brains need proper fuel to function well and that fuel comes from the food you eat.

When you fuel up with healthy foods filled with antioxidants and important vitamins and minerals, your brain is nourished properly. But if your diet is filled with sugars and processed foods (think foods in a box or fast foods), your brain has a harder time.

This image shows how much of each food group you should be eating.

ChooseMyPlate.gov

FREE RADICALS

Free radicals are chemicals that are naturally produced by our bodies as byproducts from turning food into energy. They gobble up electrons that can damage our cells and DNA. However, having too many free radicals in our bodies can be damaging. When we eat poorly, we are also ingesting free radicals. These can damage cells throughout the body in a process called oxidative stress. Free radicals are formed from various substances found in fried food, alcohol, pesticides, and air pollutants. While it's harder to control what you breathe and what's in your water, you can control the food you choose to eat. Certain foods are known as antioxidants because they combat oxidative stress. Foods that are considered antioxidants include grapes, blueberries, raspberries, strawberries, goji berries, and dark chocolate.

Foods high in sugars are harmful to your brain. Along with making it hard for your body to regulate production of insulin, sugars also increase inflammation and oxidative stress.

FOOD AND FEELING GOOD

The gastrointestinal tract is lined with a hundred million neurons. When food is being digested in the gastrointestinal tract, a neurotransmitter is produced that helps regulate sleep, appetite, and mood. That neurotransmitter is serotonin.

Serotonin is known as the happy chemical, because it contributes to our overall mood. About 95 percent of the serotonin created in our bodies is produced in our gastrointestinal tract. It makes sense that our digestive system also helps us feel better—if we are eating the right foods.

The function of the neurons in our gastrointestinal tracts is influenced by the billions of "good" bacteria that make up our intestinal environment. These bacteria protect the lining of our intestines and provide a barrier against toxins and "bad" bacteria. They limit inflammation and activate neural pathways that travel between the gut and the brain.

Studies have compared traditional diets, such as the Mediterranean and Japanese diets, to Western diets. These studies have discovered that risk of depression is 25 to 35 percent lower in those who eat a traditional diet.

Mediterranean and Japanese diets include vegetables, fruits, whole grains, and healthy fats. Dairy and red meat are limited, and weekly intakes of fish, poultry, beans, and eggs are part of the standard food being eaten. In the Mediterranean diet, olive oil and nuts are sources of healthy fats.

FITNESS FOR FEELING GOOD

A study of 1.2 million people in the United States showed that those who exercise reported having 1½ fewer days of poor mental health compared to those who don't exercise. The study, conducted in 2018, found that team sports, cycling, aerobics, and going to the gym resulted in the greatest reductions in mental health issues.

> The study also discovered that exercising for 45 minutes, three to five times a week, produced the greatest benefits.

In 2017, the results of an 11-year study of 33,908 people in Norway proved that exercise helps people avoid depression. Those who were studied did not have any signs of depression at the beginning of the study. The participants were asked about their exercise habits, and results showed that of those who responded at the start of the study that they didn't exercise, 44 percent were more likely to become depressed.

A 2017 study by Australian scientists found that exercise increases the size of the left region of the hippocampus in humans. Although the overall volume of the hippocampus did not increase, the left region grew, which is the area responsible for memory in adults. When we exercise, we produce a chemical called brain-derived neurotrophic factor, which may help to prevent age-related decline by reducing the deterioration of the brain.

How often and how intensely should you exercise to stay mentally fit? Scientists set out in 2017 to discover just that. Endorphins, the feel-good hormone, are opioids our bodies produce naturally.

NUTRITIONAL PSYCHOLOGIST

Nutritional psychology is the study of how nutrients affect our behavior and mood. A nutritional psychologist works with patients to assess their diets and track their progress. Some study the correlation between mental illness and diet. Nutritional psychologists bridge the gap between a patient's physical health and mental health. A nutritional psychologist may explore with a patient the impact of stress on their immune system or the aches and pains associated with depression. Once a patient understands the mind-body connection, a nutritional psychologist will provide strategies and guidelines to improve diets for better physical and emotional outcomes.

LOOKING AT OBESITY

The National Health and Nutrition Examination Survey shows that obesity significantly increased in both children and adults from 1999 to 2000 to the latest study in 2015–2016. The most recent study shows that 18 percent of children from ages 2 to 19 are obese, and nearly 40 percent of adults 20 years or older are obese. What might this mean for our country's mental health? What does it mean for physical health?

High-intensity interval training, which involves intense, quick cardio exercises lasting from 30 seconds to 3 minutes followed by recovery of similar time, triggers the release of endorphins in brain regions related to reward and pain processing. Moderate-intensity exercise—walking briskly, dancing, or playing tennis—also resulted in a positive mood and euphoria.

Overall, according to the U.S. Department of Health and Human Services, people should get at least 150 minutes of exercise per week. That's just 2½ hours of heart-pumping exercise for our physical health as well as our emotional and mental well-being!

How much do you exercise? If you don't currently do much, try a sport at school or through a club or find a group of friends to run or walk with. Try tennis, dance, ultimate Frisbee, or skiing. If you find something you enjoy doing, you are more likely to get the exercise your body and brain need!

SNOOZIN'

Are you getting enough sleep? Sleep experts agree that adolescents should get nine hours of sleep every night. However, according to a 2017 study, 40 percent of teens sleep less than seven hours a night. And that percentage is up significantly since the study first began in 1991.

Researchers found that the more time young people reported spending online, the less sleep they got. Teens who spent five hours a day online were 50 percent more likely to not sleep enough than their peers who only spent one hour online each day.

The scientists also found a correlation between the increased percentage of teens who got less sleep and the increase in smartphone ownership by teens. Scientific research suggests that the light wavelengths emitted by smartphones and tablets can interfere with the body's natural sleep-wake rhythm.

The short-term effects of not getting enough sleep include a lack of alertness, shortened memory, and relationship stress. Long-term effects include the risk of higher blood pressure and, ultimately, mental health issues, including depression. So, get some sleep!

MINDFULNESS MEETS SCIENCE

Do you meditate? Do you have ways that you try to practice mindfulness? Mindfulness means being fully engaged in whatever you are doing at the time.

PSYCH!

The number of scientific studies involving mindfulness has jumped from one between 1995 and 1997 to 11 between 2004 and 2006 to 216 between 2013 and 2015.

How can you be mindful? Watch this video on being mindful . . . from teens!

 mindfulness youth voices

When you are concentrating completely on a certain task, when you are emptying your mind of thoughts and focusing on the world around you, or when you are repeating a mantra, or a phrase, over and over, you are practicing mindfulness and nourishing your brain.

Here's a website for teens to learn more about being mindful.

  mindfulnessforteens

Scientists at Harvard University are studying how mindfulness can change the brain in depressed patients. Treatments for depression include antidepressants and talk therapy, but some people with depression don't respond to those treatments. Scientists have determined that mindfulness exercises not only help with physical ailments, but also help those who suffer from depression and anxiety. Well-designed mindfulness meditation programs have proven as successful as other treatment options.

GET GRITTY

Have you heard the Kelly Clarkson song, "What doesn't kill you makes you stronger"? That's a perfect definition for resilience. Sometimes called grit, resilience is the ability to recover from or adjust to difficult and even traumatic situations. It's also what we call simply getting through everyday life, which can at times feel hard, boring, or even hopeless.

Resilience is a good characteristic to have, because it means you can dig deep in yourself for the strength you need to carry through all kinds of circumstances.

Studies from the National Scientific Council on the Developing Child indicate that having one strong adult relationship is a key factor in resilience. Here's more of what the science of resilience is telling us, according to the council's report.

- Resilience comes from the interplay between a young person's internal disposition and external experience. It stems from supportive relationships, ability to adapt, and positive experiences.

- Learning to cope with manageable threats is critical for the development of resilience.

- Some children demonstrate greater sensitivity to both negative and positive experiences.

- Resilience can be developed—it's not an innate trait or a resource that can be used up.

- People's response to stressful experiences varies dramatically, but extreme adversity nearly always generates serious problems that require treatment. Resilience isn't always enough to stay healthy in the face of extreme stress.

A rubber band is resilient. So is Silly Putty. They stretch based on what is required of them and then go back to their original form. Resiliency is the ability to bounce back from a situation.

You can develop your ability to bounce back from situations in a number of ways. Here are some key strategies.

- Get together with friends and talk about what you are going through. Reach out to your parents and share what you are experiencing. You might find others have been in similar situations and might have some great advice.

TEXT TO WORLD

What examples of resiliency have you seen in yourself? Your friends? Your school?

- Be easy on yourself. Cut yourself some slack when you have had a bad experience.

- Take care of yourself. Feed your body healthy foods and get some good sleep. Bad situations can feel worse when you aren't well-rested.

- Go help somebody else. Helping others takes you away from your own problems.

- Put things in perspective. Are things really as bad as they seem?

- Break big problems into smaller ones. Small problems are easier to deal with than larger ones. That 10-page paper that's due next week? Think of it as 10, one-page assignments.

- Turn off the world. Step away from your computer, your phone, and the television and go for a walk.

Human behavior, or why we do the things we do, has been studied for thousands of years, since Aristotle wrote his book on psychology. Scientists continue to study who we are as a species and why we behave the way we do. A whole scientific community, including neuroscientists, neurobiologists, and nutritional psychologists, continues to examine why we cry, fail, and stress—ultimately so we can find our way toward smiling, striving, and singing.

KEY QUESTIONS

- **Have you tried any breathing or mindfulness exercises when facing a tough situation? Or just practiced being more in the moment?**

- **Have you been through a traumatic experience and feel stronger and more confident as a result?**

MIND THE MINDFULNESS!

Just breathe. Sounds simple, doesn't it? But, when was the last time you sat quietly for 5 or 10 minutes, just breathing? It might not be as easy as it sounds! There's a reason people call it "practicing meditation." The more you do, the more benefit you'll get from it. Let's give it a try.

Inquire & Investigate

- **Find a comfortable spot.** Whether you lie down on your bed or a sofa or sit in a chair with your head and shoulders supported, pick a quiet place with few distractions.

- **Take a deep breath through your nose.** Exhale the breath out through your mouth.

- **Put your hand on your belly.** Feel your belly rise and fall with your breath.

- **Take three breaths.** Then, take 15, 20 breaths, however many you need to take to feel a sense of calm.

- **If you're feeling stressed—in the moment— and don't have five minutes, take three deep breaths.** Even this will help center you.

- **Now, close your eyes and imagine a peaceful place.** Maybe think about the ocean waves lapping up against the shore, time and time again. You might envision the sun, rising slowly and beautifully, its pink and purple hues stretching across the horizon. Breathe, relax. Now, stand up straight, reach your hands up to that sun, and then bring your hands together, palms pressed together.

- **Meditation helps the most when you practice every day!**

To investigate more, go online and learn several simple yoga poses or sign up for a class. How do you feel after the practice? Or try putting your phone aside for an hour without looking at it. Did you feel more relaxed?

GLOSSARY

action potential: a brief pulse of electrical current that is generated by a neuron.

acute stress: most common type of stress resulting from immediate perceived threat, either physical, emotional, or psychological.

adapt: to make changes or to cope with your environment.

addiction: the condition of being addicted to a substance, thing, or activity.

adjacent: next to.

adolescence: period following the beginning of puberty during which a child develops into an adult.

adrenal glands: endocrine glands that produce a variety of hormones, including adrenaline and cortisol.

adrenaline: a hormone produced in high-stress situations. Also called epinephrine.

adverse childhood experience: traumatic events that can have negative, long-lasting effects on health and well-being.

aggression: hostile or violent behavior against another person or group of people.

amygdala: a structure in the brain that has an important role in experiencing emotions, especially fear and anger, but also positive emotions.

anatomy: the structure of a living thing.

ancestor: someone from your family or culture who lived before you.

anhedonia: the inability to experience feelings of pleasure in response to things you used to find fun and rewarding.

anthropologist: a person who studies anthropology, the study of human culture and development.

antidepressant: anything, and especially a drug, used to alleviate depression.

antioxidant: a substance in food that helps fight disease.

anxiety: a feeling of fear or uneasiness about possible misfortune. In some cases, anxiety is a mental disorder.

auditory nerve: the nerve that sends impulses from the ear to the brain.

authoritarian: a parenting style favoring complete obedience to authority instead of individual choice.

authoritative: a parenting style that is child-centered, with high expectations for behavior and strict adherence to schedule and discipline.

automatic nervous system: the part of the nervous system responsible for control of the bodily functions that are automatic, such as breathing, the heartbeat, and digestive processes.

axon: a fiber-like extension of a neuron that carries electrical signals to other neurons.

BCE: put after a date, BCE stands for Before Common Era and counts down to zero. CE stands for Common Era and counts up from zero. These non-religious terms correspond to BC and AD. This book was printed in 2020 CE.

behavior: the way a person acts or conducts himself.

behaviorism: the theory that human and animal behavior can be explained in terms of conditioning, without appeal to thoughts or feelings.

behavior: the way a person acts or conducts himself.

body mass index: a measure of a person's body fat based on weight and height.

brain stem: the lower part of the brain that connects to the spinal cord, responsible for basic life-support functions.

brain: the organ inside the head that allows you to think and feel and that controls the body.

bystander effect: a social psychological claim that individuals are less likely to offer help to a victim when other people are present, and the greater the number of bystanders, the less likely it is that one of them will help.

cancerous: affected by or showing abnormalities characteristic of cancer.

cell: the smallest unit of life.

cerebellum: the area of the brain located behind the cerebrum that helps regulate posture, balance, and coordination.

cerebrum: the largest part of the brain, where most higher-level functions and processing occur.

characteristic: a feature of a person, place, or thing, such as blue eyes or curly hair.

character: the qualities of a person or a person in a play, novel, or debate.

chemical: a substance that has certain features that can react with other substances.

chromatin: a mass of genetic material made of DNA and proteins.

chromosome: a strand of DNA that is encoded with genetic material.

chronic stress: a constant, unending stress.

circuitry: the network of interconnected neurons in the nervous system and especially the brain.

clinical depression: intense, long-term feelings of depression that should be treated by professionals.

cognitive: related to conscious and unconscious brain processes, such as perceiving, thinking, learning, and remembering information.

collaboration: to work together, a group effort.

conformity: behavior that is similar to the behavior of most of the people in a group.

conscious: perceiving or noticing with controlled thought and observation.

consensus: a general agreement.

consequence: the result of an event or condition.

control system: the nervous system, endocrine system, and reproductive and sensory systems.

coordination: the ability to use different parts of the body together smoothly and efficiently.

corpus callosum: a thick band of nerve tissue that connects the right and left hemispheres of the brain and sends messages between them.

correlation: a connection or relationship between two or more things.

cortisol: a hormone produced in response to stress.

cue: a signal.

culture: the beliefs and way of life of a group of people, which can include religion, language, art, clothing, food, holidays, and more.

cyberbullying: sending or posting negative, mean, or false content about someone else on the internet with the intent to harm them.

debunk: to prove wrong.

dementia: a group of brain diseases that cause the gradual decline in a person's ability to think and remember.

demographics: the characteristics of a population, including age, gender, education, race, religion, and ethnicity.

dendrite: a branch on a neuron that receives messages from other neurons and delivers them to the main body of the nerve cell.

density: a measure of how closely packed items are.

depression: a serious medical condition in which a person feels very sad and hopeless and often is unable to live in a normal way.

DNA: deoxyribonucleic nucleic acid. Genetic material that contains instructions that make us who we are.

dopamine: a neurotransmitter that is important in reward-motivated behavior and feelings of pleasure.

double helix: the physical shape of DNA, which looks like a ladder twisted around itself.

egocentric: thinking only of oneself, without regard for the feelings or desires of others.

embalmer: a person whose job it is to preserve a dead body.

emotion: a strong feeling, such as love or anger, about something or someone.

empathy: the ability to share the feelings of others.

endocrine system: a group of glands that produce hormones that regulate many processes in the body, including growth and metabolism.

endorphins: a group of hormones released in the brain that reduce feelings of pain and improve mood.

environment: the natural world in which people, animals, and plants live.

epigenetics: the study of biological mechanisms that switch genes on and off during an organism's lifetime.

episodic acute stress: occurs when someone experiences frequent bouts of acute stress.

estrogen: steroid hormones that promote the development and maintenance of female characteristics in the human body.

ethics: the discussion between what is right and what is wrong, or morality.

eukaryote: a class of organisms composed of one or more cells that contains a nucleus.

euphoria: a feeling of excitement and happiness.

evolution: changing gradually through time.

free radical: unstable atoms that can damage cells, causing illness and aging.

frontal lobe: the area in the front of the brain that is responsible for thinking, making judgments, planning, decision-making, and conscious emotions.

functional MRI (fMRI): techniques that allow the scientist to measure and show neural activity as visual images.

gastrointestinal: relating to the digestive system.

gender: male or female, and their roles or behavior defined by society.

gender discrimination: unequal or disadvantageous treatment of an individual or group of individuals based on gender.

gene: a segment of DNA that contains instructions for specific proteins.

genetics: the study of genes and heredity. Genes are basic units in our cells that carry characteristics from one generation to the next.

genome: the total genetic information carried by a cell or organism.

gland: an organ in the human body that secretes particular chemical substances for use in the body.

gratification: a source of satisfaction or pleasure.

gray matter: the area of the brain where synapses occur and where commands are initiated.

group dynamics: the pattern of activity that takes place in a group of people.

groupthink: the way groups sometimes make an irrational or misguided decision based on people in the group wanting to conform.

gyri: bulges of tissue on the surface of the brain.

harmony: peace and agreement.

helicopter parenting: parents taking an overprotective or excessive interest in the life of their child or children.

hemisphere: either of the two halves of the brain.

GLOSSARY

herd mentality: the tendency for people's behavior to conform to those of the group to which they belong.

heredity: the passing of traits from one generation to another.

heritability: a measure of how well differences in people's genes account for differences in their traits.

hippocampus: a small area of the brain in the temporal lobe that is responsible for emotion and memory.

homeostasis: the state of the human body being in balance.

hormones: chemicals that travel through the bloodstream to signal other cells to do their job in the body.

HPA axis: short for hypothalamic-pituitary-adrenal axis, which plays an important role in the stress response.

hypothalamus: an area of the brain that produces hormones that control many body functions, including hunger, thirst, mood, and emotion.

hypothesis: an unproven idea that tries to explain certain facts or observations.

impulsive: acting without thinking about consequences.

incentive: the possibility of a reward that encourages people to do something or work harder.

incentive processing system: structures in the brain that are responsible for motivation or craving a reward, positive reinforcement, and positive emotions such as joy and euphoria.

inflammation: part of the complex biological response of body tissues to harmful stimuli, such as pathogens, damaged cells, or irritants. It is a protective response.

inherit: to receive a characteristic or trait from a previous generation.

innate: inborn or natural.

input: the stimuli that is perceived by our senses, such as smell, sight, touch, taste, and hearing.

instinctive: a natural impulse.

insulin: a hormone produced in the pancreas that regulates the amount of glucose in the blood.

lateral prefrontal cortex: the area of the brain that plays an important role in higher-order cognitive control such as planning, behavioral inhibition, and decision-making. It is also important for motivational operations, such as processing reward information.

lenient: tolerant or relaxed, usually used when talking about someone's attitude toward discipline.

limbic system: a group of brain structures located near the inner border of the cortex that have an important role in emotion and memory.

lobe: one of the four main areas of the brain.

meditation: spending time in quiet thought.

meme: an amusing or interesting item such as a captioned picture or video that is spread widely online, especially through social media.

mental health: a person's emotional and psychological well-being.

metabolism: the processes, such as heart rate and digestion, that occur within living things in order for them to stay alive.

millennials: an age group defined by researchers as having birth years between the mid-1980s and early 2000s.

mind: the thoughts, feelings, beliefs, and intentions that arise from the brain's processes.

mindfulness: the intentional focus of one's attention on emotions and sensations in the present moment.

mood: a state of mind or predominant emotion.

moral: related to what is wrong or right behavior.

motor development: the development of a child's bones, muscles, and ability to move around and manipulate their environment.

MRI (magnetic resonance imaging): a form of medical imaging that uses high-frequency radio waves and a strong magnetic field.

myelin: a fatty material that surrounds and insulates the axons of some neurons.

neglectful: not taking care of.

nerve: a living fiber that carries information between the brain and the rest of the body.

nervous system: the communication system of the body, made of nerve cells that connect the brain and extend through the body.

neural: related to a nerve or the central nervous system.

neurobiologist: a scientist who studies the biology of the nervous system to better understand and treat neurological disorders.

neuroendocrinology: the branch of biology that studies the interaction between the nervous system and the endocrine system.

neurology: a branch of medicine that deals with the brain and nervous system.

neuron: a special cell that sends electrical and chemical messages to your brain.

neuroscientist: a scientist who studies the brain and the nervous system's structure and function.

neurotransmitter: a chemical secreted by neurons that carries signals across a synapse to another neuron.

nucleotide: a molecule containing a sugar ring, phosphate group, and nitrogen-containing base. These make up the building blocks of DNA and RNA.

nucleus: the central part of a cell that controls how it functions. Plural is nuclei.

nutrients: substances in food and soil that living things need to live and grow.

nutrition: the vitamins, minerals, and other things in food that your body uses to stay healthy and grow.

occipital lobe: an area in the back of the cerebrum responsible for visual processing.

olfactory: relating to or connected with the sense of smell.

optic nerve: the part of the eye that sends messages from the retina to the brain.

organ: a part of the body with a special function, such as the heart, lungs, brain, and skin.

organism: something living, such as a plant or an animal.

oxidative stress: an imbalance between free radicals and antioxidants in your body.

oxytocin: a hormone that makes you happy when you interact with people you like.

parietal lobe: an area of the brain near the top and back of the head, mainly involved with spatial awareness, body orientation, and attention.

Parkinson's disease: a disorder of the central nervous system that affects movement, often including tremors.

peer: a person in your group.

peer pressure: a feeling that one must do the same things as one's peers in order to be liked or respected by them.

perception: the ability to interpret information from the senses. Also a particular way of understanding or thinking about something.

peristalsis: the squeezing process of moving food through your esophagus, stomach, and intestines.

permissive: a style of parenting that allows behavior that others might not approve of.

perpetuate: to cause something to continue.

personality: the characteristics and ways of behaving that make people different from each other.

philosophy: the study of truth, wisdom, the nature of reality, and knowledge.

phosphate group: a phosphate atom bound to four oxygen atoms.

phrenology: a belief popular in the nineteenth century that personal characteristics and mental abilities could be learned from the bumps on a person's skull.

physiological: the branch of biology that deals with the normal functions of living organisms and their parts.

pituitary gland: a major gland in the endocrine system that produces hormones that control other glands and many body functions.

plasticity: the ability of the brain to change its structure and function.

Posttraumatic Stress Disorder (PTSD): a psychological reaction to a stressful event that can involve depression, anxiety, flashbacks, and nightmares.

poverty: having little money or material possessions.

predisposition: a tendency to have a particular condition.

prefrontal cortex: the area of the brain located in the anterior frontal lobe that is responsible for reasoning, planning, judgment, empathy, abstract ideas, and conscience.

protein: a nutrient that is essential to the growth and repair of tissue.

prune: to cut away, or to trim, as the brain pruning synapses in the brain.

psychoanalysis: dealing with mental and emotional problems by talking about dreams, feelings, and memories.

psychologist: a person who studies the mind and behavior.

psychology: the study of the mind and how humans think, behave, and feel.

puberty: the stage of development when a child's body starts to change into an adult body.

racial: relating to race.

rational analysis: a way of discussing subjects that doesn't include applying rigorous scientific testing.

receptor: structures that receive stimuli and produce a nerve impulse to send the information.

reciprocity: the practice of exchanging things with others for mutual benefit. Also responding to a gesture or action by making a corresponding one.

repercussion: an unintended consequence as the result of an action.

resilience: the ability to recover quickly from setbacks.

risk assessment: the process of identifying and analyzing situations that may negatively impact an individual and making judgments and choices based on the level of risk.

role model: someone who exhibits desirable behavior or habits, who serves as a model for other people.

self-conscious: feeling a heightened sense of awareness of oneself, appearance of actions.

sensory: relating to sensation or the physical senses.

serotonin: a neurotransmitter with a wide variety of functions in the body. It contributes to feelings of well-being and happiness.

short-term memory: ability to remember events or information over a shorter period of time.

signal: a process where cell-to-cell communication as well as homeostasis occurs.

social: living in groups.

social homophily: tendency for people to have relationships with those who are similar to themselves.

social loafing: the tendency of individuals to put in less effort when a large group is involved.

social structuring: to associate with friends who are like you.

socioeconomic: the interaction of social and economic factors.

spatial: relating to space and the relationship of objects within it.

GLOSSARY

species: a group of organisms that share common traits and can reproduce offspring of their own kind.

spinal cord: a thick cord of nerve tissue that links the brain to nerves in the rest of the body.

stimulus: a change in an organism's environment that causes an action, activity, or response. Plural is stimuli.

stressor: something that causes stress.

stress: pressure or strain, often due to changes in conditions or environments.

Stroop effect: a phenomenon that occurs when you must say the color of a word but not the name of the word. For example, green might be printed in red and you must say the color rather than the word.

substantia nigra: a layer of gray matter situated in the midbrain and containing the cell bodies of a tract of dopamine-producing nerve cells.

sulci: grooves in the brain's surface.

suppress: to prevent an event from happening.

susceptible: easily influenced or affected by something.

synapse: a gap between two neurons through which communication occurs.

talk therapy: a mental health treatment that involves discussing a mental or emotional disorder in order to understand and cope with it.

technology: the tools, methods, and systems used to solve a problem or do work.

temperament: the combination of mental, physical, and emotional traits of a person.

temporal lobe: an area of the brain on the side of the head involved with hearing, language, and memory.

testosterone: the male hormone sex hormone produced by the testes that encourages the development of male sexual characteristics.

tonic immobility: a temporary state of motor inhibition believed to be a response to situations involving extreme fear.

toxic: poisonous, harmful, or deadly.

trait: a specific characteristic of an organism determined by genes or the environment.

unconscious: occurring without awareness.

values: strongly held beliefs about what is valuable, important, or acceptable.

vape: to inhale and exhale the vapor produced by an electronic cigarette.

ventral striatum: part of the striatum made up of the nucleus accumbens and olfactory tubercle. The ventral striatum is involved in reward processing.

ventral tegmental area (VTA): a group of nerve cells in the midbrain responsible for releasing dopamine.

voluntary muscle: a muscle that a person controls by thinking about movement.

white matter: brain tissue beneath the cortex, made of densely packed axons that carry signals to other neurons.

yoga: a form of physical and mental exercise and meditation.

METRIC CONVERSIONS

Use this chart to find the metric equivalents to the English measurements in this activity. If you need to know a half measurement, divide by two. If you need to know twice the measurement, multiply by two.

ENGLISH	METRIC	
1 inch	2.5	centimeters
1 foot	30.5	centimeters
1 yard	0.9	meter
1 mile	1.6	kilometers
1 pound	0.5	kilogram
1 teaspoon	5	milliliters
1 tablespoon	15	milliliters
1 cup	237	milliliters

RESOURCES

BOOKS

Eagleman, David. *The Brain: The Story of You*. Pantheon Books, 2015.

Van Dijk, Sheri. *Relationship Skills 101 for Teens: Your Guide to Dealing with Daily Drama, Stress and Difficult Emotions Using DBT*, Instant Help Books, 2015.

Weeks, Marcus. *Heads Up Psychology*. DK Publishing, 2014.

RESOURCES

WEBSITES

Brain Connection:
brainconnection.brainhq.com/about

Kids' Health: kidshealth.org/en/teens

Palo Alto Medical Foundation:
pamf.org/teen/life/trauma

Child Mind Institute: childmind.org

National Child Trauma Services Network:
nctsn.org

**American Academy of Child and
Adolescent Psychiatry:** aacap.org

SELECTED BIBLIOGRAPHY

Blakemore, Sarah-Jayne. *Inventing Ourselves: The Secret Life of the Teenage Brain*. Public Affairs, 2018.

Jensen, Frances E. *The Teenage Brain: A Neuroscientist's Survival Guide to Raising Adolescents and Young Adults*. Harper, 2016.

Sapolsky, Robert M. *Behave: The Biology of Humans at Our Best and Worst*. Penguin Press, 2017.

Albert, Dustin, Jason Chein, and Laurence Steinberg. "The Teenage Brain: Peer Influences on Adolescent Decision Making," *Current Directions in Psychological Science*, April 2013, journals.sagepub.com/doi/pdf/10.1177/0963721412471347.

Dick, Danielle M., Amy E. Adkins, and Sally I-Chun Kuo. "Genetic Influences on Adolescent Behavior," *Neuroscience & Biobehavioral Reviews*, Issue 70, November 2016, sciencedirect.com/science/article/pii/S014976341630104X?via%3Dihub.

Dominique, Benjamin W., et al. "The Social Genome of Friends and Schoolmates in the National Longitudinal Study of Adolescent to Adult Health," Proceedings of the National Academy of Sciences the United States of America, January 2018, pnas.org/content/115/4/702.

Hoskins, Donna Hancock. "Consequences of Parenting on Adolescent Outcomes," *Societies*, June 2014, mdpi.com/2075-4698/4/3/506.

American Academy on Child & Adolescent Psychiatry: aacap.org/AACAP/Families_and_Youth/
Facts_for_Families/FFF-Guide/The-Teen-Brain-Behavior-Problem-Solving-and-Decision-Making-095.aspx

National Institute on Drug Abuse: drugabuse.gov/publications/
principles-adolescent-substance-use-disorder-treatment-research-based-guide/introduction

National Institute of Mental Health: nimh.nih.gov/health/topics/child-and-adolescent-mental-health/index.shtml

Pew Research Center: pewresearch.org/internet/2016/01/07/how-parents-monitor-their-teens-digital-behavior

QR CODE GLOSSARY

page 3: ceed.umn.edu/project-for-babies-videos

page 13: youtube.com/watch?v=6qS83wD29PY

page 15: youtube.com/watch?v=lRKo_dN0IME

page 17: youtube.com/watch?v=1Hmi2bVVzLQ

page 19: brainawareness.org/handouts-resources/#2

page 20: youtube.com/watch?v=ib7SS49Kk-o

page 24: psytoolkit.org/lessons/stroop.html

page 29: psychologytoday.com/us/
blog/vitality/201306/parenting-and-
the-amazing-teen-brain-part-1

page 30: abcdstudy.org/about.html

page 31: youtube.com/watch?v=-nhRPVWM9A0

page 34: fi.edu/your-brain/video/growing-up

RESOURCES

QR CODE GLOSSARY (CONTINUED)

page 36: youtube.com/watch?v=yaAuZbZSCu4

page 37: neuroscientificallychallenged.com/blog/2-minute-neuroscience-dopamine

page 39: youtube.com/watch?v=QX_oy9614HQ

page 41: youtube.com/watch?v=A9zLKmt2nHo

page 47: youtube.com/watch?v=Bln9mvpbGbw

page 55: teachertube.com/videos/little-albert-238570

page 61: kidshealth.org/en/teens/teens-talk-family-vd.html?WT.ac=t-ra

page 63: kidshealth.org/en/teens/coping-alcoholic.html?WT.ac=t-ra

page 64: youtube.com/watch?v=NjTxQy_U3ac

page 72: cyberbullying.org/get-help

page 80: scroll.in/video/843194/watch-a-crowd-of-65000-sings-bohemian-rhapsody-perfectly-while-waiting-for-a-green-day-concert

page 81: youtube.com/watch?v=ft7mwyiPyIo

page 82: rotary.org/en/get-involved/interact-clubs

page 84: youtube.com/watch?v=X0V4mNMu8E0

page 85: youtube.com/watch?v=1-U6QTRTZSc&feature=youtu.be

page 89: youtube.com/watch?v=quQr6X1Q58I

page 90: youtube.com/watch?time_continue=25&v=v-t1Z5-oPtU

page 91: kidshealth.org/en/teens/school-stress.html?WT.ac=hottopic#catfeeling-sad

page 92: kidshealth.org/en/teens/stress.html

page 94: youtube.com/watch?v=7HzYOxHNhNU

page 94: kids.frontiersin.org/article/10.3389/frym.2017.00071

page 95: youtube.com/watch?time_continue=122&v=IQYh6dKVmxs

page 98: kidshealth.org/en/teens/school-counselors.html#catfeeling-sad

page 107: youtube.com/watch?v=kk7IBwuhXWM

page 108: mindfulnessforteens.com

INDEX

INDEX